T0077557

Statistical Analysis and Decision Making Using Microsoft Excel

Grace Edmar Elizar del Prado

PARTRIDGE

A Penguin Random House Company

Copyright © 2014 by Grace Edmar Elizar del Prado.

ISBN:	Softcover	978-1-4828-9102-7
	eBook	978-1-4828-9101-0

All rights reserved. No part of this book may be used or reproduced by any means, graphic, electronic, or mechanical, including photocopying, recording, taping or by any information storage retrieval system without the written permission of the publisher except in the case of brief quotations embodied in critical articles and reviews.

Because of the dynamic nature of the Internet, any web addresses or links contained in this book may have changed since publication and may no longer be valid. The views expressed in this work are solely those of the author and do not necessarily reflect the views of the publisher, and the publisher hereby disclaims any responsibility for them.

"Statistical Analysis and Decision Making Using Microsoft® Excel" is an independent publication and is not affiliated with, nor has it been authorized, sponsored, or otherwise approved by Microsoft Corporation.

To order additional copies of this book, contact
Toll Free 800 101 2657 (Singapore)
Toll Free 1 800 81 7340 (Malaysia)
orders.singapore@partridgepublishing.com

www.partridgepublishing.com/singapore

Contents

About the Author

Grace Edmar Elizar-del Prado finds fulfilment in and draws her passion from various social-research activities. Economic theories and statistics applications constantly marvel at her inquisitive mind. With a bachelor's degree in economics from the Ateneo de Davao University, Philippines, and a master's degree in economics from the Ateneo de Manila University, Philippines, Ms. del Prado has developed her deep appreciation to data analysis and profound enthusiasm in understanding decision-making processes.

Through time, she has presented a number of papers, with a few winning "best paper" awards. Since 2006, her work institution has honoured her with Research Excellence Awards. She won an International Award for Research Advocacy from the Philippine Association of Institutions for Research and Asian Research Advocacy Award from the International Association of Multidisciplinary Research.

She is an associate professor of the Western Visayas College of Science and Technology (WVCST) and is designated senior researcher to chair the Social Science Research Center.

Acknowledgments

To my late husband, Raymundo, this manuscript is for your honour and respect.

To Ram Anthony and Mahasara Patricia, I love you.

To Dr. Renato Alba, President Emeritus of WVCST, my gratitude.

To Trafford Publishing, students, and friends, thank you.

To my clients, take at least a copy.

In the name of Allah, I humbly offer this work to God's glory alone and to my deep appreciation to Maryam (the mother of Jesus).

Introduction

Information is an important input to sound decision-making. Insufficient data will not provide enough insight, but so much information—untreated and unorganized—will not offer the needed insight either. In this information age, the increasing volume of information may not be optimally utilized if there is no tool that can make the analysis comprehensible to many people.

Two forms of information exist: data in quantitative and in qualitative structure. These are not different. For example, a $400.45 income is a quantitative, continuous data, with income as the variable. This can be transformed into a "low-income bracket" to put a particular meaning to the quantitative value. This new reclassified data is now called qualitative data.

World organizations and institutions gather vast information on various indicators. These data require treatment before they can be interpreted. High-end studies use very powerful software to speed up data analysis, but for simpler studies by local institutions and smaller firms, Microsoft Excel is a good yet powerful statistical software they can use.

This manuscript is split into four modules. Module 1 presents how data can be described. Module 2 introduced various event-probability calculations. A study might require an inferential treatment to form a conclusion, and module 3 contains such an approach. Finally, module 4 provides tools that make management easy and simple. Analyses and decision-making processes are made easier with the use of Microsoft Excel 2000.

Module 1

Describing Quantitative-Qualitative Statistical Data

M ovements of periodic quantities, such as total imports from other countries from 1980 to 2010 and increases in family sizes over the last ten years, can be analyzed by graphing. This is to describe trends. In analyzing trend lines, it is suggested to pay extra attention to the slope of the line and on the changes that occurred from point to point. Major events that have happened corresponding to the changes in points that are rising or those that are declining might be noted. And significant policies that must have been implemented during those changes might be identified.

Example 1.1. US total imports from China from 1985 to 1991 (in million dollars) are depicted in the following table. The researcher wants to describe the trends. What would the researcher find out?

Table 1.1 US Total Imports from China,[1] 1985–1991, in Million Dollars

Year, x	1985	1986	1987	1988	1989	1990	1991
Cost of imports, y	3862	4771	6293	8511	11990	15237	18976

Table 1.1 provides costs of imports from 1986 to 1991. To see clearly the trend over time, graphing the data might be of great help. In Excel, you may do the following:

Steps in Excel

1. Enter data in two columns. Highlight the data set.
2. Click **Insert,** choose **Chart,** and then select **Scatter** (the same procedure for other graphical figures).
3. Results are shown in Chart 1.1.
4. Edit your work to your desired presentation.

Chart 1.1 US Total Imports from China, 1985–1991

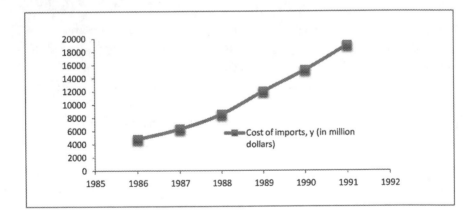

---

[1]   E. Connally, D. Hughes-Hallett, A. Gleason, et al., "Fitting Curves to Data," *Functions Modeling Change: A Preparation for Calculus* (John Wiley and Sons, Inc. USA, 1998), 187.

Possible Description of Chart 1.1

The US cost of imports from China is increasingly rising from 1986 to 1991 (as shown in the mounting volumes of goods bought each year). These are estimated by the growing sizes of (imaginary) triangles formed from point to point. The trend can be due to, but not limited to, China's increasing efficiency in labor and capital resource use in the 80, owing from some favorable consequential effect of communist economic system that resulted to having cheaper goods and competitive resource prices for the global market.

Example 1.2. A Filipino garment exporter has to decide which country to expand business to: the United States or Japan. The data provided to him are the Philippine export trend between these two countries from 1975 to 2006. The data are as follows:

	Philippine Direction of Trade, 1975-2006 (in million US dollars)												
Exports Total	1975	1977	1979	1980	1983	1986	1988	1990	1992	1995	2000	2002	2004
United States	663.1	1113.3	1390	1593.6	1792.6	1658.3	2512	3103.6	4107.3	6217	11406	8691	7209
Japan	858.3	731.7	1214.2	1540	983.7	874.5	1415.5	1622	2019.6	2740	5609	5293	7983

Graphing the data set, the graph looks like this:

Chart 1.2 Philippine Direction of Trade, USA and Japan, 1975–2006

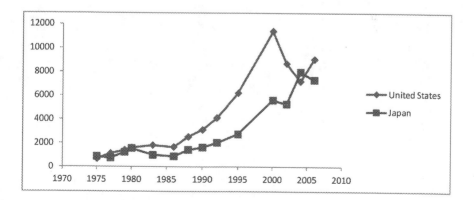

What possible information does graph 1.2 present?

One can see that in general there is a growing and enlarging demand for Philippine goods from the United States than from Japan. Glancing at the downtrends, the executive may specifically look at the current fluctuations of demand for Philippine garments in American markets, the factors affecting the declining demand, other robust indicators within the company, and the quality of competition in the industry, before he can assure strong market stability.

Magnitude Comparison

For a sectional data set, one may compare varying magnitudes to describe lead, speed, or productivity, or any point of interest given information.

Following the same Excel steps previously presented, a data set may be remapped using different presentation styles. The example that follows portrays a bar graph for fish production output in various localities in Iloilo Province, Philippines.

Example 1.3. Students in community development of the Western Visayas College of Science and Technology, Iloilo City, Philippines, wanted to measure the average weekly fish catch of villagers in the province and identify which village produces the highest and lowest fish catches. Chart 1.3 shows the bar graph. What observations can be drawn from the data set?

Chart 1.3 Average Weekly Fish Catch in Iloilo Province, Philippines, 2008–2009

(Balino 2010)

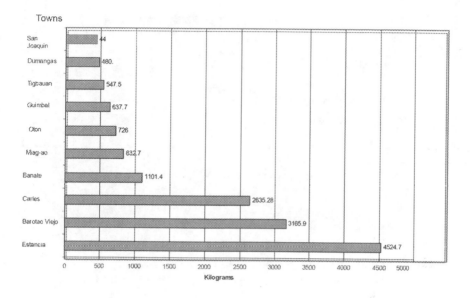

Steps in Excel

1. Enter data. Highlight them.
2. Click **Insert**, choose **Bar,** select **2D,** and then click **OK.**

Observations

Iloilo Province is gifted with fish resources. Fishermen's average weekly catch is at least forty-four kilograms of different fish species. Estancia is the biggest fishing ground in the province.

Overall, however, production is uneven. Some coastal towns produce more while other towns produce very little. Because income relates to the volume of the fish catch, it can be hypothesized that incomes of fisher villagers are also uneven.

Example 1.4. A qualitative, variable "exchange" has three different classifications. The figure below shows its magnitudes. It is shown that the exchange over the counter has the highest frequency.

Chart 1.4

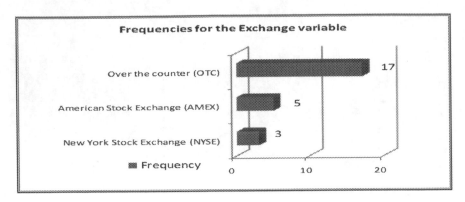

Frequencies for the Exchange variable

(Anderson, Sweeney, and Williams 2006)

Steps in Excel

3. Enter data. Highlight them.
4. Click **Insert**, choose **Bar**, select **3D**, and then click **OK**.

Example 1.5. Third-world economies identify if anti-poverty programs are effective. This is measured by finding the change in the proportion of underweight children under five years old after feeding programs, intensive education series, family-planning intervention, and many other complementing programs have been implemented. For Asia, the actual data of selected countries are presented in the table that follows.

a. Present in another table the transformed information that show how large the reduction in proportion of underweight children under five years old is.
b. Graph the changes and make a little description.

Table 1.5a Prevalence of Underweight Children under Five Years of Age

(Asian Development Bank 2012)

Prevalence of Underweight Children Under Five Years of Age				
	(%)			(%)
	%	Earliest Year	%	Latest Year
Afghanistan	44.9	(1997)	32.9	(2004)
Bangladesh	61.5	(1990)	41.3	(2007)
Cambodia	42.6	(1996)	29.0	(2011)
China, People's Rep. of	12.6	(1990)	3.4	(2010)
India	59.5	(1990)	43.5	(2006)
Indonesia	29.8	(1992)	19.6	(2007)
Pakistan	39.0	(1991)	31.3	(2001)
Philippines	29.9	(1990)	20.7	(2008)
Thailand	16.3	(1993)	7.0	(2006)
Viet Nam	36.9	(1993)	20.2	(2008)

Answers

a. To find the change in proportion, take the difference between the earliest years and the latest years. Take note of the year difference in each country. To compare magnitudes annually, the change in proportions will be divided by the number of years specified.

For example, in Afghanistan, the change in proportion of underweight children under five years old is 12 percent. This change has been realized between 1997 and 2004, which is seven years inclusive. Therefore, to calculate for the annual change, 12 percent is divided by seven years, and the resulting annual reduction in underweight children aging below five years old is 1.71 percent.

The transformed table is as follows:

Table 1.5b.

Asian Economies	Change within specified years (%)	Years	Average reduction per year (%)
Afghanistan	12	7	1.71
Bangladesh	20.2	17	1.19
Cambodia	13.6	15	0.91
China, People's Rep. of	9.2	20	0.46
India	16	16	1.00
Indonesia	10.2	15	0.68
Pakistan	7.7	10	0.77
Philippines	9.2	18	0.51
Thailand	9.3	13	0.72
Viet Nam	16.7	15	1.11

b. The graph presents the annual reduction in the proportion of underweight children under five years old. Among the countries, Afghanistan is able to achieve a national goal of reducing poverty through the reduction of the proportion of underweight children below five years old.

Steps in Excel

1. Enter the data in table 1.5.
2. On another column, subtract the values in the "earliest years" from the "latest years" to get the change over time by clicking "=" first on the operation window next to the **fx** button before proceeding to the subtraction method.
3. To calculate for the annual change, divide the values computed in number 2 to the number of years' difference between "earliest years" and "latest years."

4. To graph these values, make two columns. The first column contains the names of the economies, and the second column contains the average-reductio-per-year column.
5. Highlight these columns, click **Insert**, and choose **Column** charts.
6. Right-click on the bars and choose **Add Data Labels**.
7. You may add an inside title by clicking **Insert** and then choosing **Text Box**. Write, "**Average Annual Reduction in the Proportion of Underweight Children under Five Years Old (%).**"
8. The results are as follows.

Chart 1.5. Average Annual Reduction in the Proportion of Underweight Children under Five Years Old (%).

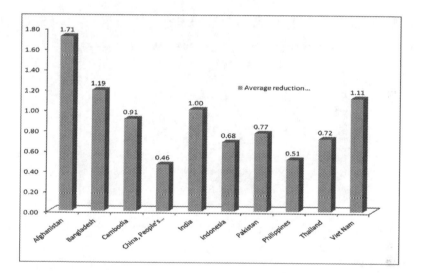

Distribution Depiction

Different shapes of data sets portray certain mass convergences, tendencies, or preferences of certain groupings of points in question. Measures of symmetry are sometimes classified as the third central moment, with mean and variance as the first and second central moments and kurtosis as the fourth moment. Measures of lopsidedness of a distribution or skewness include the normal, right-skewed, and left-skewed distributions.

The *normal distribution* is a theoretically expected distribution of certain sets of data where the mean and median are the same. When they are equal, none of the data deviated away from the specified mean value. Under a normalized scale of –3 to +3 standard deviations, the mean and median value are zero. If so, then this distribution is said to be symmetrical or zero skewed.

However, if mean exceeds the median value, the *distribution is right skewed*. This happens because unusually high values affect the value of the mean. Right-skewed distribution has its tail longer to the right. The opposite of this is the *left-skewed distribution*. A distribution is left skewed if median exceeds the mean value. Left-skewness arises when the mean is reduced by some extremely low values. Left-skewed distribution has its tail longer from the left.

Figures A, B, and C. Different Shapes from Three Data Sets

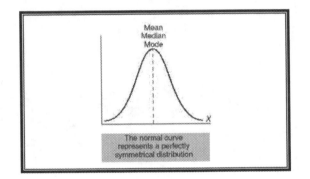

(http://www.southalabama.edu/coe/bset/johnson/lectures/lec15.htm)

a) **Symmetrical**

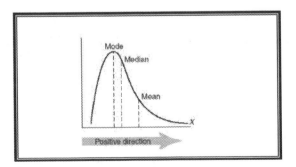

(http://www.southalabama.edu/coe/bset/johnson/lectures/lec15.htm)

b) Right Skewed

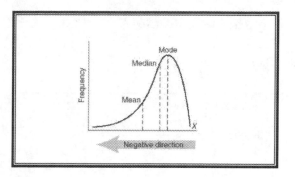

(http://www.southalabama.edu/coe/bset/johnson/lectures/lec15.htm)

c) Left Skewed

Excel readily provides numerical values of descriptive statistics that determine the distribution of data.

Example 1.6. Students' scores in a sixty-item summative test in basic economics:

24, 45, 34, 25, 38, 35, 22, 35, 23, 25, 23, 55, 54, 56, 57, 50, 22

Steps in Excel

1. Enter data in a column. Click **Data** and choose **Data Analysis.** Select **Descriptive Statistics** and click **OK.**
2. In the **Input Range** window, enter the range of the data set, by highlighting the data set in step 1.
3. Check **Labels in the First Row**, **Summary Statistics**, and **New Worksheet** in the output options. Then click **OK.**

The output is presented below.

Table 1.6 Summary Statistics of Students'

Performance in Basic Economics Course

scores in 60 item test in Basic Economics	
Mean	36.65
Standard Error	3.28
Median	35.00
Mode	25.00
Standard Deviation	13.51
Sample Variance	182.62
Kurtosis	-1.54
Skewness	0.39
Range	35.00
Minimum	22.00
Maximum	57.00
Sum	623.00
Count	17.00

Table 1.6 shows that the distribution is right skewed because the value of skewness is positive (0.39). This could be doubly checked by comparing the mean and median values. True enough, the mean is larger than the median.

Example 1.7. Students' scores in a sixty-item summative test in Basic Statistics:

55, 45, 34, 25, 47, 45, 32, 35, 56, 55, 50, 55, 54, 56, 57, 50, 22

The results are shown in the table that follows.

Table 1.7 Summary Statistics of Students'

Performance in Basic Statistics Course

scores in 60 item test in Basic Statistics	
Mean	45.47
Standard Error	2.80
Median	50.00
Mode	55.00
Standard Deviation	11.55
Sample Variance	133.51
Kurtosis	-0.52
Skewness	-0.89
Range	35.00
Minimum	22.00
Maximum	57.00
Sum	773.00
Count	17.00

Here, the mean is smaller than the median and the index for skewness is negative. Hence, the distribution is left skewed.

Comparing Skewness Results of the Two Tables

Assuming that the same group of students took tests in basic economics and basic statistics, the data reveal that more students find economic theory difficult to grasp than statistical theory shown in the higher frequency of getting lower scores in basic economics.

Spreads Identification

Two symmetrical polygons that share the same central tendencies may differ in spread or dispersion. When the distribution is less variant, data points converge closely to the average, while on the contrary, if it is more variable, the dispersion is large. Figure D shows the difference.

Figure D. Distributions Having the Same Mean with Different Spreads

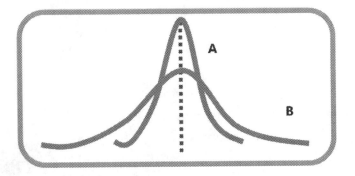

A and **B** polygons share the same mean value. They also have symmetrical shapes. The only difference is that A is convergent to the mean while B spreads away. A distribution with less variation portrays a more stable condition compared to that which is more dispersed.

This information is important to note as a less divergent data set connotes homogeneity in quality contained in a set. The more spread there is in a distribution implies the presence of a significant variety in quality among the items contained in the set.

Distributions like **B** polygon have kurtosis numerical value of less than three (platykurtic), and polygons like **A** have kurtosis numerical value of more than three (leptokurtic).[2] The normal distribution shape has a kurtosis of three, called mesokurtic. Kurtosis is defined as the measure of tallness and fatness of a probability distribution function.

Example 1.8. Table 1.8 shows the sales performance of two competing gasoline companies in five outlets. Which company shows inter-outlet sales stability? The summary statistics show the answer.

---

2   Damodar Gujarati, "A Review of Basic Statistical Concepts," *Essentials of Econometrics 2nd ed.* (Singapore: Irwin McGraw-Hill, 1999).

Table 1.8 Daily Sales of Two Competing Gasoline Companies in Five Stations (in Thousand Pesos)

Outlet Station	Petrol Company	Flying High Company
A	77	82
B	79	82
C	86	84
D	86	85
E	92	87

Possible Interpretation of the Summary Statistics

Largely, both companies converge to Php 84,000 daily sales. This is indicated with the skewness index being closed to zero. Both data sets have leptokurtic heights showing fatter and shorter tails.

Summary Statistics of Two Competing Gasoline Companies

Sales of Petrol		Sales of Flying High	
Mean	84.00	Mean	84.00
Standard Error	2.70	Standard Error	0.95
Median	86.00	Median	84.00
Mode	86.00	Mode	82.00
Standard Deviation	*6.04*	*Standard Deviation*	*2.12*
Sample Variance	36.50	Sample Variance	4.50
Kurtosis	-1.29	Kurtosis	-0.96
Skewness	0.11	Skewness	0.52
Range	15.00	Range	5.00
Minimum	77.00	Minimum	82.00
Maximum	92.00	Maximum	87.00
Sum	420.00	Sum	420.00
Count	5.00	Count	5.00

However, in terms of dispersion, Petrol sales are more dispersed than that of Flying High. Flying High has s.d. = 2.12 while Petrol has s.d. = 6.04. Interestingly, all stations in Flying High have obtained sales levels within the ₱5,000 range (82 to 87). This is a rather smaller range deviation. Based on this, Flying High has shown to have more stable inter-outlet operations than that of Petrol.

Steps in Excel

1. Enter data. Click **Data.** Choose **Data Analysis.**
2. On the **Data Analysis** tools, choose **Descriptive Statistics**.
3. In the **Input Range** window, enter the data set by highlighting the data-set area. Click **Labels on the First Row, Summary Statistics, Confidence Level for Mean. And then click OK.**

To install the **Data Analysis** button,

1. Open the Microsoft Excel Office button on the upper-left portion of the worksheet.
2. Click **Excel Options**; look for the **Add-Ins** button from the left-side column.
3. At the bottom part, enter **Excel Add-Ins**. Click **Go.**
4. On the **Adds-In Available** tools, click **Analysis ToolPak** and **Analysis ToolPak-VBA.** Click **OK.**

Example 1.9. Table 1.9 presents the growth rates of Singapore and Hong Kong from 2003 to 2011. Which country shows a more erratic growth rate?

Table 1.9a Growth Rates of Singapore and Hong Kong, 2003–2011

(The World Bank 2012)

Years	Singapore	Hong Kong
2003	5	3
2004	9	9
2005	7	7
2006	9	7
2007	9	6
2008	2	2
2009	-1	-1
2010	15	7
2011	5	5

Possible Answer: Variance indicates stability of growth rates across time. From table 1.9B, Singapore's variance (or s.d.^{2}) is higher than Hong Kong's. This implies that internal and external volatilities have influenced Singapore's growth rate more than Hong Kong's.

Table 1.9b Growth Rates of Singapore and Hong Kong, 2003–2011

Singapore		Hong Kong	
Mean	6.67	Mean	5.00
Standard Error	1.55	Standard Error	1.04
Median	7.00	Median	6.00
Mode	9.00	Mode	7.00
Standard Deviation	4.64	Standard Deviation	3.12
Sample Variance	21.50	Sample Variance	9.75
Kurtosis	0.56	Kurtosis	0.21
Skewness	0.09	Skewness	-0.86
Range	16.00	Range	10.00
Minimum	-1.00	Minimum	-1.00
Maximum	15.00	Maximum	9.00
Sum	60.00	Sum	45.00
Count	9.00	Count	9.00
Confidence Level(95.0%)	3.56	Confidence Level(95.0%)	2.40

Qualitative Flows Directions

Example 1.10. The following table presents the various trading partners of Southeast Asian economies, including the specific years each is trading with the partners and its growth-rate average.

a. Why are the data on this table called qualitative data?
b. What economies are trading with the Philippines, and what economy does the Philippines trade with the most?

Table 1.10 Export Trading Partners, Selected Southeast Asian Countries, 1990–2007

Country	Export Trading Partner	Trading Years	Geometric Mean
Philippines	Thailand,		17.5
	Malaysia		20.59
	China	1990-2007	43.30
	Singapore		21.31
	Hong Kong		18.85
	United States		06.81
Indonesia	Germany		09.52
	Australia		15.36
	Malaysia		21.17
	Korea	1990-2007	11.98
	China		17.54
	Singapore		12.93
	United States		09.21
	Japan		04.86
Singapore	Korea		36.96
	Thailand		19.84
	United States	1990--2007	13.11
	Malaysia		27.93
Vietnam	Thailand	1990-2007	20.44
	Malaysia		20.86
	Germany		28.76
	Japan		44.37
	United States	1990-2005	18.57
	China		
Myanmar	Germany		17.19
	Japan	1990-2007	14.97
	India		18.43
	Thailand		26.50
Thailand	Singapore	1990-2007	11.39
	United Sates		08.46
Malaysia	Korea		10.69
	Thailand		14.11
	Hong Kong	1990-2007	14.51
	China		22.17
	Japan		08.24
	Singapore		08.86
	United States		12.44

Answers

a. The data are in qualitative form because the elements presented are in words. In particular, the Philippines' trade directions reach to only six economies. The Philippines trade with the United States of America, Hong Kong, Singapore, China, Malaysia, and Thailand. Contrary to many expectations that the United States is its major economical trade partner, the table reveals that the Philippines has traded most with China (at a rate of 43.3 percent).

b. Geometric mean is the only quantitative information present. This gauges the average growth rate of trading activities of economies from 1990 to 2007.

Steps in Excel

1. Make two columns. One is for the various economics the Philippine economy is trading with, and the other is for the geometric mean values.
2. Highlight the data set but exclude the titles from highlighting.
3. Click **Insert**, choose **Bar,** and select **2D Option**. You may want to explore other options to fit the desired outcome.
4. Point the cursor to any of the bars and right-click to choose **Add Data Labels.**
5. You may delete the label box and the line to make your presentation clearer.

Chart 1.10 Philippine Trading Partners, Trade Geometric Growth Rate, 1990–2007

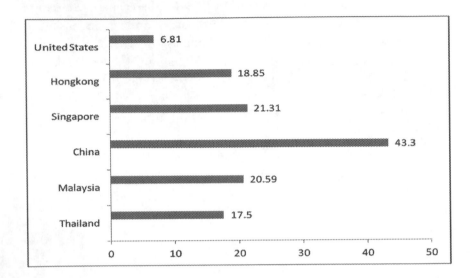

Example 1.11. The following table shows the employment sectors that absorb labour force. (Asian Development Bank 2012). Which sector is employing labor the most?

Table 1.11 Philippine Employment Distribution, Sectors, in Thousands, Calendar Year 1990–2007

LABOR FORCE[b,c] *thousand, calendar year*																
Employment Sectors	1994	1995	1996	1997	1998	1999	2000	2001	2002	2003	2004	2005	2006	2007	2008	2009
Agriculture	11286	11147	11645	10416	10091	10774	10181	10850	11122	11219	11381	11572	11662	11785	12030	12044
Manufacturing	2539	2617	2696	2720	2715	2759	2745	2906	2869	2941	3061	3097	3053	3059	2926	2894
Mining	111	107	113	122	114	97	108	103	113	104	118	119	139	149	158	166
Others	11097	11806	12734	13106	13711	14111	14419	15295	15958	16372	17054	17401	17761	18567	18974	19958

Answer: Despite the objective of increasing growth via manufacturing, the Philippines has remained an agricultural economy. The chart shows that next to other sectors, agriculture employs the highest number of individuals. The trend remained the same up to the recent years.

Chart 1.11 Labour Employment Distribution in the Philippines

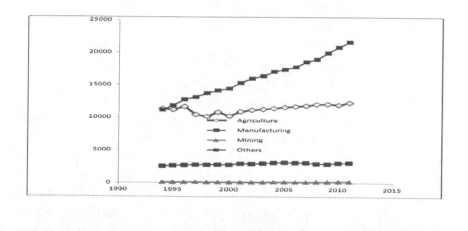

Frequency Counts Description

Because qualitative data are usually in categories, classifications, qualifications, and qualities, describing frequency counts as part of treatment provides ample information about a data set. Take the following fictitious example.

Example 1.12. An administration wants to assess classroom performance of Dr. Generoso Domingo VI, a teacher in English 107. This performance is extracted from students' evaluations. Will the administration promote the teacher? Table 1.12 presents the summary.

First, understanding what information surrounds table 1.12 is necessary. It is an evaluation summary of thirty students. Dr. Domingo's class meets from 9:00 to 10:30 a.m. Tuesdays and Thursdays. Eleven good qualities expected of a teacher are identified, and Dr. Domingo is rated based on these qualities.

Perception evaluation is useful if revealed information drawn is independent from respondent to respondent. Perception independently verified denotes some approximation about the truth in question. This is why randomness is important to eliminate the element of bias. The column heading contains the teacher's qualities and the row heading contains the students' numbers.

Instead of describing Dr. Domingo's qualities in words, the English department coded the description in numbers. If the student feels that the quality needs improvement, the score is a 1; if mediocre, 2; if fair enough, 3. If the teacher exudes a quality level beyond the average expectation of the student, the student scores a 4, and if an exceptional quality is found, 5. Note, however, that it is necessary for respondents to have a uniform idea of what mediocre, fair, exceptional, etc., mean. Otherwise, there would be thirty different meanings for each quality.

How does one treat table 1.12? To treat data as numbers does not provide any meaning. In addition, vertical average scoring is not valuable either. Why is that? It is because the values are in descriptions. Take the first column. Student 1 thinks that Dr. Domingo has just enough of quality 1. However, he/she also thinks that the teacher needs improvements in quality 8, although Dr. Domingo is rated exceptional in qualities 4 and 11. What is the overall quality of Dr. Domingo for student 1?

One matter to note is that the administration is interested in all students' perception of Dr. Domingo and not on student 1's overall perception. The summary data, therefore, is read horizontally, not vertically. The concern is how many students in this class find Dr. Domingo at least *fair enough* in qualities. How manifest are these good qualities to students? This information guides the administration to what intervention is necessary or what promotion scheme is due to Dr. Domingo for the next school year.

Table 1.12 Evaluation Summary of Dr. Generoso Domingo VI, English 107, 11 Expected Qualities, 30 Evaluators, First Semester, 2011

Teacher Dr. Generoso Domingo VI							Subject: English 107				9:00 – 0:30 am. Tuesdays and Thursdays																		
Student #	1	2	3	4	5	6	7	8	9	10	11	12	13	14	15	16	17	18	19	20	21	22	23	24	25	26	27	28	29	30
Teacher's Qualities																														
1	3	4	2	5	3	5	2	4	2	3	3	3	3	5	4	5	3	3	3	3	5	3	3	5	3	3	5	3	3	3
2	4	5	3	5	3	4	2	3	1	4	2	4	2	5	5	4	4	2	4	2	5	4	2	5	4	2	5	4	2	4
3	3	4	3	5	3	5	3	4	2	3	3	3	3	3	3	5	3	3	3	3	3	3	3	3	3	3	3	3	3	3
4	5	5	2	5	3	5	4	3	1	2	4	2	4	2	4	4	2	4	2	4	2	2	4	2	2	4	2	2	4	2
5	3	4	3	5	4	5	5	4	2	3	5	3	5	4	5	4	3	5	3	5	4	3	5	4	3	5	4	3	5	3
6	4	4	4	5	5	5	4	5	3	5	3	5	3	5	4	5	5	3	5	3	5	5	3	5	5	3	5	5	3	5
7	2	4	3	5	3	5	4	5	3	5	2	5	2	5	5	5	5	2	5	2	5	5	2	5	5	2	5	5	2	5
8	1	5	4	5	4	3	5	5	4	2	2	2	2	4	3	4	2	2	2	2	4	2	2	4	2	2	4	2	2	2
9	4	5	5	5	5	4	4	2	5	1	3	1	3	5	4	5	1	3	1	3	5	1	3	5	1	3	5	1	3	1
10	4	4	5	5	5	4	3	3	5	2	4	2	4	3	5	5	2	4	2	4	3	2	4	3	2	4	3	2	4	2
11	5	3	5	1	4	5	2	2	5	1	4	1	4	4	3	3	1	4	1	4	4	1	4	4	1	4	4	1	4	1

1 = needing improvement; 2 = mediocre; 3 = fair enough; 4 = above the usual expectations; 5 = exceptional

To achieve this is to count how many students rated 1, 2, 3, 4, and 5 in each quality. This is finding the *modal* response. **Mode** is found to be a better average measure for qualitative data.

Steps in Excel

1. Enter raw data. Make another matrix adjacent to the sheet matrix. This is to allow easy Excel computations.
2. In that matrix, put the headings 1, 2, 3, 4, 5—one number classification in each cell. Move the cursor under the "1" heading. Click **fx** and on the **Select a function** window, click **COUNTIF.**
3. On the "range" window, click the cursor first. Once the cursor is on it, go back to the worksheet and highlight the first row containing all the data points. The highlighted range will be registered on the range window.
4. Click the criteria window, and click 1 if the point of interest is to count how many rated the teacher 1. Before OK is clicked, the answer is already shown. Click **OK.**

5. Do the same in the next column under 2, and proceed by doing the same steps for numbers 3, 4, and 5. I suggest repeating the process as though it is the first time, because if the formula is only copied for the next cells, there are instances that the encoder forgets to check the formula in the formula bar and the results will be wrong. Be careful with this step, as this is about giving justice to the one being evaluated.

6. Once the first cell has all filled up, simply copy them, and paste the results to the remaining cells underneath. The results are shown on the following page. The adjacent matrix is highlighted.

Teacher's Qualities																														1	2	3	4	5	f
1	3 4 2 5 3 5 2 4 2 3 3 3 3 5 4 5 3 3 3 5 3 3 5 3 3 5 3 3 3																													0	3	17	3	7	27
2	4 5 3 5 3 4 2 3 1 4 2 4 2 5 5 4 4 2 4 2 5 4 2 5 4 2 5 4 2 4																													1	3	3	18	7	20
3	3 4 4 5 5 3 5 3 4 2 3 3 3 3 3 5 3 3 3 3 3 3 5 3 3 3 3 3 5																													0	1	24	2	3	29
4	5 5 2 5 3 5 4 3 1 2 4 2 4 2 4 4 2 4 2 4 2 2 4 2 2 4 2																													1	13	2	18	4	16
5	3 4 3 5 4 5 5 4 2 3 5 3 5 4 5 4 3 5 3 5 4 3 5 4 3 5 3																													0	1	10	8	11	29
6	4 4 4 5 5 5 4 5 3 5 3 5 3 5 4 5 5 3 5 3 5 5 3 5 5 3 5																													0	0	8	5	17	30
7	2 4 3 5 3 5 4 5 3 5 2 5 2 5 5 5 5 2 5 2 5 5 2 5 5 2 5																													0	8	1	2	17	22
8	1 5 4 5 4 3 5 5 4 2 2 2 2 4 3 4 2 2 2 4 2 2 4 2 2 4 2 2 2																													1	15	3	8	4	14
9	4 5 5 5 5 4 4 2 5 1 3 1 3 5 4 5 1 3 1 3 5 1 3 5 1 3 3 1																													8	1	7	4	18	21
10	4 4 5 5 5 4 3 3 5 2 4 2 4 3 5 5 2 4 2 4 3 2 4 3 2 4 2																													0	8	6	10	6	22
11	5 3 5 3 4 5 2 2 5 1 4 1 4 4 3 3 1 4 1 4 1 4 4 1 4 4 1 4 1																													9	2	3	12	4	19

How would the administration award good qualities? Benchmarks can be of help. This is one example:

1. A monetary increase of fifty pesos is added to the salary for every "good quality" that is evident. A good quality is evident if at least 50 percent of the students rated the teacher *fair enough* or better. Such an increment takes effect the following school year.

2. Since the salary incentive is dependent on the performance of the teacher, the salary incentive fluctuates, depending on the faculty-evaluation results.

To count how many students find Dr. Domingo at least fair enough in qualities, the last three columns (3, 4, 5) can be added per row. If totals exceed 50 percent, then a fifty-peso salary adjustment is granted. The same process is done for the rest of the quality rows. Unfortunately, in quality 8, Dr. Domingo got *fair enough* by less than 50 percent (fourteen totals for 3, 4, 5), thus no reward is given for this particular quality.

Overall, Dr. Domingo is eligible to enjoy a ₱500 (550 – 50) salary adjustment in the next school year.

Here, it is observed that evaluation marks are important but requiring some careful study. A question asking if the teacher is willing to give extra time beyond the designated official hour may be revised, because staying beyond official time can be vaguely interpreted as staying late even for non-academic purposes. This can lead to serious immorality and sexual harassment issues if unchecked.

Another ambiguous question is whether the teacher shows kindness. Kindness can be doubly interpreted as diploma-mill corruption. If straight—giving failing grades to lazy students—the teacher is rated unkind. Well, this is all wrong.

Many administrators are forcing statistics to provide overall ratings. Conceptually, this is incorrect, because a teacher is not a static reality. There are areas he/she may be good at and areas where he/she needs improvement. It is rather illogical to average the best qualities and poor qualities and end up in the middle—*fair-enough* quality. Should it be reinforced, then it is best to go back to the benchmark. If the faculty is rated exceptional by 100 percent of student raters, then he/she is highly promotable if 95 percent; 99 percent means very promotable, and so forth.

Relative Changes Comparison

Frequency Counts Comparison

Aside from tallying occurrences, the researcher may compare relative occurrences across various elements under a variable. For simple frequency distribution, one can fairly provide an intelligent description about shares and proportion, like that in table 1.13.

Example 1.13. The demand for bottles for various uses—on beers, soft drinks, and medicine—is determined by ABC Bottle Company for the year-end of 1999. Present the information in chart form.

Table 1.13 Demand for Bottles for Various Uses—Beers, Soft Drinks, and Medicine, ABC Bottle Company, 1999 (Hypothetical Data)

Bottles	Frequency	Percentage (%)
Beers	1500	21.43
Soft drinks	2100	30.00
Medicine	3400	48.57
Totals	7000	100,00

Table 1.13 contains qualitative data because the classification "bottles" contains three different classification elements—beers, soft drinks, and medicine. The next two columns identify the number of bottles being demanded for each classification and the distribution percentage of all the bottles demanded respectively. Almost 50 percent of the total demand goes to medicinal use. Does this indicate health deterioration among people? Health researchers may look at this scenario more closely.

To present the comparative frequency of the demand for bottles in Excel, the steps are the following:

Steps in Excel

1. Enter data. Highlight them. In this case, exclude the third column and the cell with **"Totals."**
2. Click **Insert** and choose the **Column Bars.**
3. Pick the bar type of your choice and click **OK.**
4. In the heading part, replace the default heading with **Demand for Bottles for Various Uses—Beers, Soft Drinks, and Medicine, ABC Bottle Company, 1999.**
5. On the layout chart tools, click **Primary Horizontal Axis Title** and write **Various Bottle Uses.**
6. Repeat the procedure, and do the same for **Primary Vertical Axis Title** and write **Frequency.**
7. The resulting chart looks like chart 1.13.

Chart 1.13

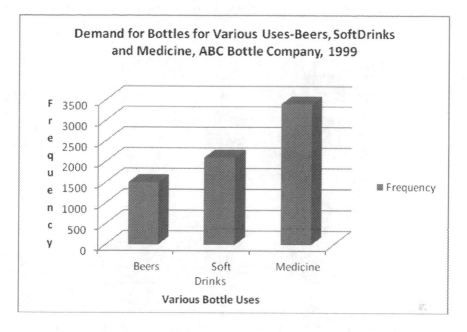

Demand for Bottles for Various Uses-Beers, SoftDrinks and Medicine, ABC Bottle Company, 1999

Frequency Changes Comparison

A dding more information to Table 1.13 expands our ability to understand data. Relative changes in information across years could present an even sharper contrast. Consider the next example.

Example 1.14

Table 1.14 Demand for Bottles for Various Uses—Beers, Soft Drinks, and Medicine, ABC Bottle Company, 1990 and 2010, Comparative Statistics

Bottles	1990	2010	Change
Beers	1500	2150	650
Soft drinks	2100	3420	1320
Medicines	3400	2890	-510
Totals	7000	8460	

Chart 1.14 Demand for Bottles for Various Uses—Beers, Soft Drinks, and Medicine, ABC Bottle Company, 1990 and 2010, Comparative Statistics

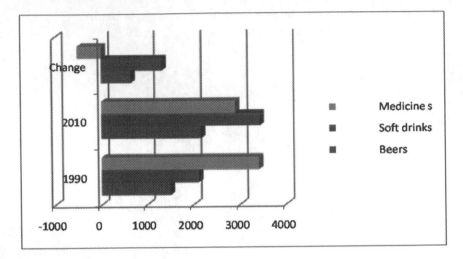

Adding new information changes the original perception. The demand for bottles for medicine use dropped significantly compared to other uses. On the "Change" grouping, the right side of the graph denotes a positive change while the left side denotes a decrease in quantity. Here, the previous guess about health deterioration indicated by relatively high demand for medicine is no longer a strong proposition.

Steps in Excel

1. Enter data in a worksheet. Highlight the areas to be graphed. Exclude the totals.
2. Click **Insert**, choose **Bars,** and select the **Bar Type** of choice.

Relative Performance Comparison

Frequency counting allows researchers to compare relative frequency magnitudes. Such simple approach can be useful, especially for companies that are in constant competition with other players in the industry. Refer to the example that follows.

Example 1.15. According to *Beverage Digest*, Coke Classic, Diet Coke, Dr. Pepper, Pepsi Cola, and Sprite are the five top-selling soft drinks (*The Wall Street Journal Almanac* 1998).[3] Present information graphically.

Table 1.15 Frequency Distribution of Fifty Soft Drink Purchases, 1998

Soft Drink	Frequency
Coke Classic	19
Diet Coke	8
Dr. Pepper	5
Pepsi Cola	13
Sprite	5
Total	50

As is, the data fail to hint about market strengths. If transformed into proportions, results trigger a different view. Chart 1.15 shows why.

Clearly, the Coke Classic market share of 38 percent proves its strength and dominance in the industry. But while this looks very promising, it is yet an unsafe position. Pepsi Cola, the closest competitor, might take a more aggressive action to overtake Coke Classic.

Steps in Excel

1. Enter Data. Highlight the area. Click on **Insert,** and choose **Pie** chart.
2. Right-click and click **Add Data Labels**.
3. This time, it is better to format labels in percentages. Click **Format Data Labels,** and check the **Percentage** button.

---

[3]   D. Anderson, D. Sweeney, and T. Williams, "Descriptive Statistics 1: Tabular and Graphical Methods," *Essentials of Statistics for Business and Economics, 2nd ed.* (USA: South-Western College Publishing, 2000).

Chart 1.15 Relative Strengths of Five Leading Soft Drinks

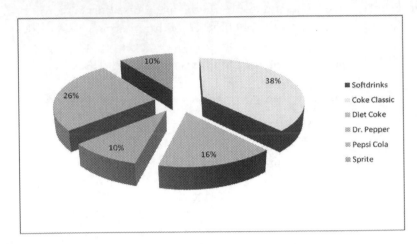

Interpretation

1. The pie graph presents the relative market share of the various soft-drink products. Instantly, market dominance of Coke Classic is identified.
2. The chart also identifies the needs for Dr. Pepper and Sprite to take aggressive marketing to expand market.

Example 1.16. Local executives took the National Preparedness Test. This is to check how updated they are in responding to various conditions. Present data in a doughnut graph. To what attribute do men show the strongest ability? What about women?

Table 1.16 Relative Strengths of Local Mayors in the Philippines (Hypothetical Data)

Gender	Mathematical ability (average rating)	Verbal Competence (average rating)	Analytical Skills (average rating)	Psychological and Ethical Balance (average Rating)
Men	95	78	79	89
Women	83	85	78	92

Chart 1.16 Doughnut Presentation of Mayors' Relative Strengths

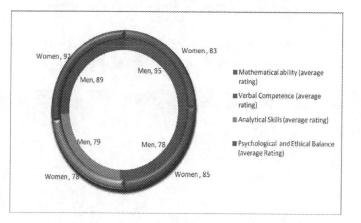

Possible Interpretation of the Doughnut Graph

Overall, male mayors score higher in math and women mayors in psychological and ethical balance. On the other hand, in verbal skills, the women mayors achieve better and in analytical ability, both fare the same. To further strengthen these claims, additional treatments may be necessary.

Steps in Excel

1. Enter data. Highlight raw data in the sheet. Click **Insert**, and choose **Doughnut** graph.
2. To improve the graph, you may add data labels by clicking **Data Labels** and formatting it by clicking **Values** and **Data Series.** Then click **OK.**

Example 1.17. Most governments commit themselves to addressing corruption. Corruption is an obstacle to progress, as most transactions are lost under the table—unrecorded, unbalanced, and unreconciled.

In the 2010 Corruption Perception Index published by Transparency International, it is reported that nearly three-quarters of the 178 countries score below five in the index, indicating a serious corruption problem permeating across countries, destroying the ethical standards of societies. The following table shows the Honesty Index of Southeast Asian countries. What country in Southeast Asia maintained national integrity and practised honesty in all transactions throughout the entire system?

Table 1.17a Honesty Index (1-Corruption Index) of Selected Countries in Southeast Asia, Selected Years, 1990–2010 (Asian Development Bank, various years)

	1990	1995	2000	2005
Malaysia	5	5.3	4.9	5.1
Philippines	2.7	2.6	2.3	2.4
Lao People's Democratic Republic	1.6	1.4	1.6	1.8
Cambodia	2.3	2.4	2.6	2.4
Thailand	3.6	3.5	3.2	3.7
Singapore	8.5	9.1	9	8.9

Steps in Excel

1. Enter data in a worksheet. Highlight the data area.
2. Click **Insert**, choose **Column,** click the column of your choice, and then click **OK.**
3. If you want to reformat, click the chart area.
4. Click **Design,** and choose **Switch Row/Column.**
5. Click anywhere to finalize your output.
6. The output is shown below.

Table 1.17b Honesty Index (1-Corruption Index) of Selected Countries in Southeast Asia, Selected Years, 1990–2010

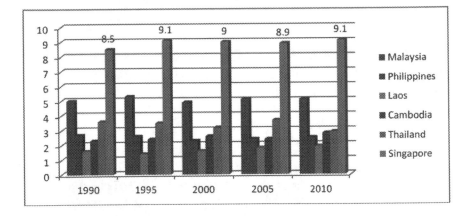

Possible Interpretation of the Graph

Singapore, a progressive economy, maintained cleanliness in all its operations—government or private. Following Singapore, though not very close, is Malaysia. The Philippines has not shown any improvement since the '90s. The Republic of Laos is ranked the lowest in the list. Why do you think so?

Example 1.18. The following data present the distributions and spreads of two groups. Describe them graphically.

Table 1.18a Scores on Aggression Measure, Model and Non-Model Group (Hypothetical Experiment)[4]

Model Group	Non-Model Group
3	1
4	2
5	2
5	3
5	3
5	3
6	4
6	4
6	4
7	5

Steps in Excel

1. Enter Data. Click the **Data** button. Choose **Data Analysis.**
2. Choose **Descriptive Statistics.** Click on the **Input Range** window, and then go back to the data set and highlight them. The highlighted cells will be registered in the window.

---

[4]   Paul Cozby, "Descriptive Statistics," *Methods on Behavioral Research, Sixth Edition* (California, USA: Mayfield Publishing Company, 1997), 178.

3. Click **Summary statistics**, Tick on the **Labels on the First Row,** and click on all other buttons if desired. Then click **OK.**
4. The output is shown below.

Table 1.18b Descriptive Statistics of Model and Non-Model Groups

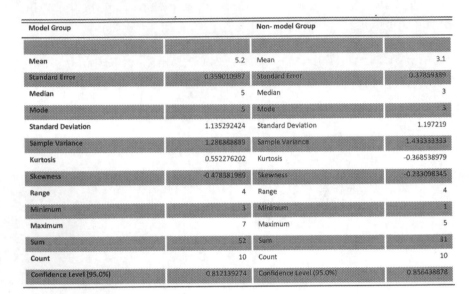

Model Group			Non-model Group		
Mean		5.2	Mean		3.1
Standard Error		0.359010987	Standard Error		0.37859389
Median		5	Median		3
Mode		5	Mode		3
Standard Deviation		1.135292424	Standard Deviation		1.197219
Sample Variance		1.288888889	Sample Variance		1.433333333
Kurtosis		0.552276202	Kurtosis		-0.368538979
Skewness		-0.478381989	Skewness		-0.283098345
Range		4	Range		4
Minimum		3	Minimum		1
Maximum		7	Maximum		5
Sum		52	Sum		31
Count		10	Count		10
Confidence Level (95.0%)		0.812139274	Confidence Level (95.0%)		0.856438878

Answer

The model-group distribution is negatively skewed, and the non-model group is positively skewed. To construct a polygon, the given data are transformed into frequency distribution. This transformed distribution will be the one being graphed.

Steps in Excel

1. Make three columns—scores, model group, and non-model group. Under **Scores**, enter all possible scores—1 to 7.
2. Tally how many scored 1 to 7 for both groups.

3. Click **Insert,** choose **Scatter,** and click the **Scatter with Smooth Lines and Markers** option.
4. The results are found below.

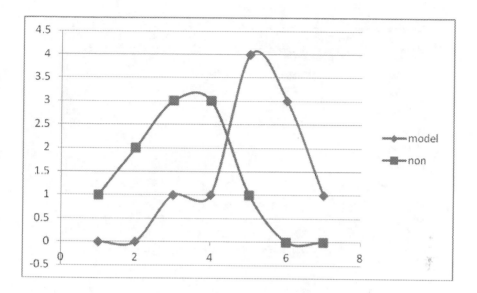

The distributional difference is now clearer. The model group is more left skewed, as many subjects were getting higher scores. In contrast, the non-model group is positively skewed where scores of many converged to lower values.

Example 1.19. The data below present the economic growth rates of Southeast Asian economies from 1990 to 2009 at various base years in their own local currencies.

a. What country is growing the fastest?
b. What description can be said about the regional growth? Comment or suggest.

Table 1.19 Economic Growth Rates, Southeast Asian Countries, 1990–2009 at Various Base Years at Local Currencies

(Asian Development Bank, various years)

Country	Growth Rate (%)	
Vietnam	7.44	
Lao People's Democratic Republic	22.54	
Thailand	4.21	
Philippines	3.68	
Myanmar	36.64	
Malaysia	8.74	
Cambodia	28.38	
Brunei Darussalam	1.82	
Indonesia	11.78	
Singapore	5.93	

Answers

a. Myanmar came out the fastest-growing economy during the period. To see which country grows the fastest, graphing the data might be the best strategy. The results are the following:

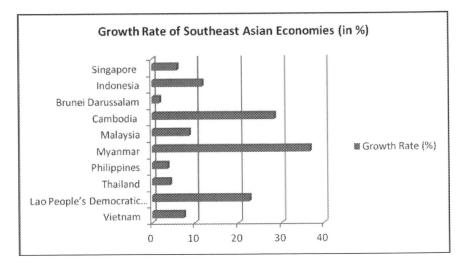

b. Growths in the region are uneven. The region may consider economic and political integration to socially profit from the expected beneficial consequences of cooperation. More trading cooperation and access to government supports projects like climate disaster control and intensive training on small-scale income, generating projects that mutually benefit societies alike.

Module 2

Calculating Probabilities Using Quantitative-Qualitative Statistical Data

One important aspect of statistical information is its use in calculating probabilities. Probabilities usually operate when one makes predictions or gives intellectual opinions about the likely occurrence of certain events meaningful to the individual, to a certain group, to a particular community or specific sector, or to humanity as a whole. Three basic approaches on probability are *a priori* classical probability approach, empirical classical probability approach, and subjective probability approach.

A priori classical probability approach — The probability of success is based on a prior knowledge of the process involved. When all outcomes are equally likely, the chance of occurrence is defined as follows:

Probability of occurrence = s/N

Where;
s = number of outcomes in which the event is expected to occur (success)
N = total number of possible outcomes

Empirical classical probability approach — With this approach, the chance of occurrence depends on the information taken from an observed data or survey. Examples of this could be the proportion of individuals in a survey who revealed preference to a particular politician and actually voted to that preferred politician, or who work and study full-time while accepting odd jobs during spare time, etc.

Subjective probability approach — The probability assigned by the individual is solely based on his/her own experiences, opinions, and analysis, which may be different from the perspectives of others. This is likely applied when outcomes could not be determined empirically. An example includes a hunch about the probability of a golden toilet bowl business to succeed. Since there are no golden toilet bowls sold, empirical probability is indeterminable.

A priori probability approach — One must use logic to determine what outcomes of an event are possible in order to determine the number of ways these outcomes can occur.

Example 2.1 (*a priori probability approach*). What is the probability of rolling a 3 or a 4 with a balanced die?

Answer: In a balanced die, there are six sides. Each side assumes a number from 1 to 6. Since the probability of getting one side up is 1/6, the probability of getting either a 3 or a 4 will give

$$\mathbf{s = 2} \text{ and } \mathbf{N = 6,} \text{ so:} \qquad s/N = 2/6 \text{ or } 1/3.$$

Example 2.2 (*empirical probability approach*). If two of twenty loaf breads to be shipped have expired and four of the twenty are randomly chosen for inspection, what is the probability that none of the expired ones will be chosen?[5]

---

[5] Similar examples are found in this source: J. Freund and F. Williams, *Elementary Business Statistics: The Modern Approach* (New Jersey, USA: Prentice Hall, Inc., 1982), 116.

Solution. The number of ways one can select four out of twenty items is given by

$$\begin{bmatrix} 20 \\ 4 \end{bmatrix} = 4{,}845$$

The number of ways that none of the expired will be selected is given by

$$\binom{2}{0} = 1.$$

The number of ways four will be selected from the fresh bread is given by

$$\binom{18}{4} = 3{,}060.$$

Hence, $s/N = \dfrac{\binom{2}{0}\binom{18}{4}}{\binom{20}{4}} = \dfrac{3{,}060}{4{,}845} = 0.6315.$

Steps in Excel for Computing Combinations

1. Click the **fx** button. Choose **All** under the **Select a Category** prompt. Select the function **Combine.** Click **OK.**
2. In the first window, enter the total number of items, such as 20.
3. In the second window, enter the number ways in which a selection is made, such as 4.
4. Click **OK** and the answer must be 4,845. Do the same for the rest.

Figure 2.1 The Excel Environment Showing the fx Button

Example 2.3. There were 230 respondents in a social survey on climate change. The distribution of the respondents according to age is given as follows:

Frequency Distribution According to the Ages of the Respondents

Number of Respondents	Ages
35	Under 18 years
105	18 up to less than 30 years
35	30 up to less than 50 years
40	50 up to less than 70 years
15	70 and over

Given this distribution, what is the probability that if a questionnaire was chosen at random, it would be from the respondent who would be under eighteen, thirty up to less than fifty years old, or seventy and over?

a. What is the probability that it would be from a respondent over seventy years old?

b. What is the probability that the respondent would be thirty up to under fifty and fifty up to under seventy years?

Answers: To calculate the probability that a respondent would be under eighteen years old, thirty up to less than fifty years old, or seventy and over, the approach is this:

1. Get the frequency of each category.
   under 18 years = 35
   30 up to less than 50 = 35
   70 and over = 15
2. Add them together and divide it with the total number of respondents. *s/N*=
3. *s/N* = 85/230 = 0.3695
4. Therefore, the probability that a respondent would be either under eighteen or thirty up to less than fifty or seventy and over is 36.95 percent. To calculate the probability that it would be from a respondent over seventy, the approach is the following:
   a. Get the frequency of 70 and over and this is 15.
   b. *s/N* = 15/230 = 0.0652 or 6.52 percent.
   c. Therefore, the probability that it would be from a respondent over seventy years old is 6.52 percent.

The probability that it would be coming from a respondent who is thirty up to less than fifty *and* fifty up to less than seventy years is **zero**, since these two events are mutually exclusive. It means that a respondent could not fall in two categories. Note the use of the word *and*. This connotes that two conditions happen simultaneously. Naturally, this is impossible.

Example 2.4. The following table presents the various income ranges and the number of families falling in each range. What description or implication can one give to the distribution? What is the probability that if one information sheet is taken, it is from the respondent whose income is less than ₱15,000?

Table 2.4 Frequency Distribution on the Number of Families in Each Income Class

Income Range	Frequency (no. of families)
< 15,000	8
15,000 - <25,000	14
25,000 - < 35,000	18
35,000 - < 45,000	15
45,000 - < 55,000	10
55,000 - < 65,000	8
65,000 - < 75,000	5
75,000 - < 85,000	3

Answer

1. The distribution is ***right skewed.*** This implies that there are more families falling under lower income brackets. The probability that it will be taken from a respondent whose income is less than ₱15,000 is **0.098** (found by 8/81, where 8 is the frequency of the income bracket earning less than ₱15,000, and this is divided by the total number of families across incomes. The number of families is 81).

Probability Measurements of Qualitative Data

Probabilities are values from 0 to 1, with 0 being a perfect nonoccurrence and 1 a perfect occurrence. However, even with data that are in categories and classifications, probabilities can also be computed based on frequency counts.

Example 2.5. A local executive wants to find the employment status of all adults who have completed the requirements for a college degree. The objective is to calculate the overall area's strengths and comparative advantages as well as its weaknesses and opportunities. The following table presents the records:

	Employed	Unemployed	Totals
Males	580	20	600
Females	240	268	508
Totals	820	288	1108

From this, some information can be unearthed.

1. The relative strength of the area is 74 percent (total employed/ total adult population).
2. The rate of weaknesses is around 26 percent (total unemployed/ total adults/population).
3. The likelihood for a female who finished college to be unemployed is 53 percent (i.e., P [unemployed | females] = [268/508]).
4. The likelihood for a male college graduate to be unemployed is 3 percent (i.e., P [unemployed | males] = [20/600]).
5. The probability of a citizen to be both female and unemployed is 24 percent (i.e., P [female ∩ unemployed] = [268/1,108]).

With these, the local executive can make a few useful assessments. He can assess current conditions via target conditions. If the employment rate target is at least 90 percent, then the employment difference from the target is 16 percent (90 percent to 74 percent). In addition, jobs available are mostly male intensive, making employment skewed against the women sector. Therefore, women-intensive employment may be prioritized. Examples could be those in the assembly sectors like watch and cell phone jobs, in manufacturing like those in garments production and design, or in banking and finance-related work like those in rural banks and lending corporations.

Employment generates multiplier effects. Employment in the primary sectors stimulates demand for other normal goods and services produced like leisure, beauty, and health. Services in spa and massage clinics, beauty parlours, restaurants, food chains, and comedy bars will also be stimulated. Jobs for auxiliary services like security, maintenance, and cleanliness will also be opened. Supply effects on food will also be encouraged. See, even with this simple information, the local executive will be guided as to what priorities to take during the entire term.

There are problems when frequency distribution is contingent with the circumstances. The relative frequencies are random and not fixed. Let us take the following example.

Example 2.6. The issue on the RH bill has created opposing opinions that divide the society in general. A study wants to find out whether being for or against the legislation has anything to do with beliefs espoused by various religions. Samples of 2,913 mothers from across the country were interviewed. Results are presented in table 2.6.

Table 2.6 Relative Choices of Stakeholders, Religion, Philippines 2010 (Hypothetical Data)

	Catholic Christians	Muslims	Non-Catholic Christians	Non-Christians and Non-Muslims	Totals
For the RH Bill	290	120	389	500	1299
Against RH Bill	370	199	456	589	1614
Totals	660	319	845	1089	2913

What does the table say? First, find that variables are both stochastic. Of the 2,913 identified samples, the frequencies on opinions and religions depend largely on the responses of the respondents; hence, they are all on chance. This is an example of a contingency table where both the row and column totals are contingent to circumstances. How to proceed with analysis?

If the objective is *only to present probabilities and likelihood* but not to test statistically the observed frequencies, one can do expectations analysis. The steps are these:

a. Present column and row totals like in the given example.
b. Divide the row totals by overall total and multiply it with the column totals. For example, for the first row total of 1,299, divide this by 2,913 (1,299/2,913) and then multiply the quotient with the column total, 660. So it would be (1,299/2,913) * 660 ≈ 294. This means that it is expected that 294 of the Catholic Christians

would vote for the legislation and 366 ([1,614/2,913] * 660) would be against the legislation.

c. From among the Muslims, it is expected that 142 ([1,299/2,913] * 319) of them would be for the legislation and 177 ([1,614/2,913] * 319) would be against it, and so forth.

d. The likelihood for any Catholic Christians to opt for the legislation is 290/660 = 0.44 or 44 percent or P (for legislation | Catholic Christian) = P(L∩CC)/P(CC) = 290/2,913 * 2,913/660 ≈ 0.44. One may do similar presentations for other information.

Example 2.7. A sample of one thousand respondents were asked whether they planned to purchase a large TV. Twelve months later, the same respondents were asked again whether they actually purchased the television (Levine 1999). The results are as follows:

Table 2.7

	Actually Purchased		
Planned to Purchase	Yes	No	Totals
Yes	200	50	250
No	100	650	750
Totals	300	700	1,000

From the table, how will the researcher form his or her market report on television demand?

Possible Answer

The demand for large televisions can be influenced by factors other than early planning. From the table, it is observed that at the start of the survey, one-fourth (250/1,000) of the total respondents planned to purchase a large television. This proportion can be used to measure the probability of selecting a respondent who planned to purchase a large TV. After twelve months, the actual overall demand proportion changed. It went up to 30 percent (300/1,000), a rise of 5 percent.

Moreover, 80 percent (200/250) of those who planned to purchase a large television actually bought one, while 20 percent of them changed their minds. On the other hand, a little more than 60 percent (200/300) of those who bought a television really had planned ahead to buy one. This left a little more than 30 percent of the purchases that are unplanned. This value is the other-factors effect. Though it is quite unclear what made respondents change their mind, it is still more obvious that buying behaviour can always change at will. A more aggressive marketing operation will perhaps induce more changes in demand in favour of buying a large television.

Steps in Excel

1. To find ratios, proportions, or the quotient of two numbers, click first the equal sign (=) in any cell. Then enter the numerator value and press the division sign, followed by the denominator value. Click **OK.**
2. In all mathematical operations, the use of the equal sign is used prior to the operation to signal Excel that the value entered will be treated as a number and not as text.

Example 2.8. The table below shows the population and crime-rates matrix of selected political divisions in Region VI, Philippines. If you were a political analyst helping the police regional director, how would you describe the information to him/her?

Table 2.8 No. of Crimes Committed, Average Monthly Crime Rate, Solution Efficiency Rate, Population, Region VI, Philippines, 1992				
Political Division	Total Number of Crimes Committed (f) 2011	Average Monthly Crime Rate (%)	Solution Efficiency Rate (%)	Population in 2010
Aklan	564	13.57	44	535,725
Antique	301	5.73	44	546,031
Capiz	468	7.27	31	719,685
Guimaras	91	7.75	55	162,943
Iloilo	749	4.75	48	1,805,576
Negros Occidental	924	4.91	26	2,396,039

Possible Answer: One may reclassify the data by describing population as highly populated and less populated and crime rates as high and low, and then proceed to simple interpretation of the data.

Table 2.9

Crime Rates	Population 1 Million and Over = Populated	Less Than 1 Million = Less Populated
High if 5 percent and over		Aklan, Antique, Capiz, Guimaras
Low, if otherwise	Iloilo, Negros Occidental	

It is observed that areas with populations greater than one million people have crime rates lower than 5 percent. This figure looks very encouraging, but you should not be deceived by it. This is so, because the large denominator value stretches the numerator down, generating overall lower crime rates. Hence, concluding about peace and order on the basis of crime rates may not be a satisfactory gauge. In fact, the raw data reveal otherwise. In table 2.10, Iloilo registered the second highest in the total number of crimes committed and came out most efficient in resolving crime issues. In fact, Iloilo leads in the solution efforts to crime problems.

These rates also represent expectations for future possibilities. For instance, the solution efficiency rate of 44 percent may suggest that in Aklan, on average, a particular crime committed will be solved at most 44 percent of the time.

Table 2.10 No. of Crimes Committed, Average Monthly Crime Rate, Solution Efficiency Rate, Population, Region VI, Philippines, 1992					
Political Division	Total Number of Crimes Committed (f) 2011	Average Monthly Crime Rate (%)	Solution Efficiency Rate (%)	Population in 2010	Actual Solution Efficiency
Aklan	564	13.57	44	535,725	248
Antique	301	5.73	44	546,031	132
Capiz	468	7.27	31	719,685	145
Guimaras	91	7.75	55	162,943	50
Iloilo	749	4.75	48	1,805,576	360
Negros Occidental	924	4.91	26	2,396,039	240

Probability Based on Distributions

In some situations, problem cases do not give raw data. Only salient information is presented. Microsoft Excel can still be of great help in calculation.

A. The Binomial Distribution

Example 2.11. A manufacturer of automobile tires reports that among a shipment of five thousand sent to a local distributor, one thousand are slightly blemished. If one purchases ten of these tires at random from the distributor, what is the probability that exactly three with be blemished (Walpole 1993)?

Answer: 0.2013
Steps in Excel

   3.   Click the **fx** button. From the function choices, locate **Binomdist.**

4. Based on the problem given, enter the necessary information on each window.
5. The answer is registered before **OK** is clicked.

When does a distribution become a binomial distribution? Discrete random variables take a binomial distribution when the interest is on *x* **successes** and *n − x* **failures** in *n* **trials**. For example, one is interested in getting fifty out of one hundred mail questionnaires sent to respondents, or thirty out of forty-seven smaller outlets of a beverage company to expand to Europe or 87 percent passing rate of the CPA Board Exam in a particular year. Discrete, random variables are variables that take only a finite number of values or whole numbers (as opposed to continuous values).

The probability of obtaining x successes out of n independent trials is given by

$$f(x) = \left(\frac{n}{x}\right)(p)^{x*(1-p)n-x.}$$

Example 2.12. The probability that a patient recovers from a rare blood disease is 0.4. If fifteen people are known to have contracted this disease, what is the probability that at least ten survive (Walpole 1993)?

Answer: What is asked is that, of the fifteen patients, at least ten, eleven, twelve, thirteen, fourteen, or fifteen will survive. Find the probability in each of these values and then find the sum. The answer is 0.033833303.

Steps in Excel

1. Calculate the probability for each x.
2. Add the probabilities. To add addends, highlight the values and then click the Σ sign. A green arrow points at the encoded data and the answer. The Excel environment is found in the chart below.

Example 2.13. If the probability is 0.30 that any convicted corrupt government official will be removed from office, what is the probability that in a random sample of eight convicted corrupt government officials, five will be removed from office?

Solution: x = 5; n = 8; p = 0.30

$$f(3) = \binom{8}{5} (0.30)^5 (1 - .30)^{\,8-5} = 0.036675$$

Answer: 0.046675 is the probability that five will be removed from office from the eight convicted corrupt government officials.

Steps in Excel

1. Click the **fx** button. On the **Select a function** choose **BINOMDIST** and click **OK.**
2. On the **Numbers** window, enter 5(as this is what is asked from the problem i.e the number of officials who be removed from the office).

3. On the **Trials** window, enter 8 (as this is the total number of independent trials).
4. On the **Probability_s** window, enter 0.30 (as this is the probability stated in the situation).
5. On the **Cumulative** window, enter **False.** (We enter False if we want to get the probability mass function and True if we want to get the cumulative distribution function
6. Before **OK** is clicked, the answer is presented just below the windows.

B. The Poisson Distribution

Poisson distribution is often used to approximate a binomial distribution when *n* is large and *p* is small. The distribution follows this formula:

$$f(x) = \frac{np^x e^{-np}}{x!} \qquad \text{For } x = 1, 2, 3 \dots$$
$$e = 2.71828$$

Example 2.14. A department store has several payment lanes for customers but designates one express lane to serve those buying at most ten items. The probability that a customer in this store will use the express lane is 0.10. Find the probability that among five randomly selected customers, there is zero, one, two, or three who will use the express lane.

Solution

n = 5; p = 0.10; x = 0, 1, 2, 3
For *f*(0) = 0 = 0.59049
For *f*(1) = 1 0.32805
For *f*(2) = 0.0709
For *f*(3) = 0.0081

Example 2.15. The average number of radioactive particles passing through a counter during one millisecond in a laboratory experiment is four. What is the probability that six particles enter the counter in a given millisecond (Walpole 1993)?

Answer: 0.1042

Steps in Excel

1. Click the **fx** button. Locate **Poisson.**
2. Based on the problem given, enter the necessary information on each window.
3. The answer registers before **OK** is clicked.

Example 2.16. Records show that the probability is 0.0006 for a runner to collapse in a one-hundred-metre dash competition. Find the Poisson approximation of a binomial distribution to find the probability that among 1,500 runners, at least two will collapse.

Solution: $np = 1,500(0.0006) = 0.9$
$e = 2.71828$
$x = 2, 3, 4 ... 1,500$

To find the probability that *at least two runners* will collapse, it is easier to solve for the probability when $f(0)$ and $f(1)$ are calculated, the sum of which are deducted from 1.

$f(0) = 0.4065$
$f(1) = 0.3659$

so

$1 - (0.4065 + 0.3659) = 0.2276$ *found by*
$1-0.4065-0.3659=0.2276$

Steps in Excel

1. Click the **fx** button. Select **Poisson** among the function options.
2. Click **OK.** Enter **0** in the x window.
3. For the **mean** window, enter **np** value. In the cumulative window, enter **False.**
4. Do the same for x = 1.

Example 2.16. If, for example, three customers will enter a department store at six in the afternoon,

a) What is the probability that in a given minute, two customers will enter?
b) What is the probability that more than two will enter a department store?

Answer

a) For x = 2, the probability is 0.2240.
b) For x >2, one needs to calculate the probability of x = 0, x = 1, and x = 2. Then add their probabilities. To find the complement of it, deduct the sum of probabilities from 1. The difference is the probability that more than two will enter a department store. The answer is 0.57681.

a) Excel result for x = 2

b) Excel result for x >2

Example 2.17. A hospital had three thousand deliveries each year. If these happened randomly around the clock, one thousand deliveries would be expected between the hours of midnight and 8.00 a.m. Since this is when many staffers are off duty, it is important for the hospital to ensure that there will be enough people to cope with the workload on any particular night

   a.   On how many days in the year would five or more deliveries be expected?

55

Answer: The average number of deliveries per night is 1,000/365, which is 2.74. From this average rate, the probability of delivering 0, 1, 2, etc., babies each night can be calculated using the Poisson distribution. Some probabilities are

- $P(0)$ 2.74^0 $e^{-2.74}/0! = 0.065$
- $P(1)$ 2.74^1 $e^{-2.74}/1! = 0.177$
- $P(2)$ 2.74^2 $e^{-2.74}/2! = 0.242$
- $P(3)$ 2.74^3 $e^{-2.74}/3! = 0.221$

Continue calculating for $P(4)$ and then add their probabilities. The total probability is 0.856898. Deduct this value from 1 to measure the $P(X \geq 5)$. The resulting probability is 0.143102. Multiplying this by 365 days a year gives the number of days where at least five deliveries in a night are expected.

C. The Hypergeometric Distribution

To illustrate the multiplication rule for independent events, sampling with replacement is usually used. Binomial distribution, on the other hand, is correctly used with sample replacement. For example, the probability of getting two aces from fifty-two cards is (4/52) * (4/52) = 0.0059, because after getting a card, it was returned to the deck. This consequently makes the second drawing independent from the first draw.

Oppositely, consider a different scenario. Suppose that the probability that a burglar alarm system will be installed in a warehouse is 0.90 and the probability that the burglar alarm will be installed and will decrease the number of burglaries is 0.60. What then is the probability that if the burglar alarm is installed, the number of burglaries will decrease? The probability is 0.67, found by (0.60/0.90). Here the situation provides a situation called conditionality, and that is the installation of a burglar alarm. These events, therefore, are not independent.

To introduce a probability distribution that applies when sampling without replacement is done, take the example that follows.

Example 2.18. Among a department store's sixteen delivery trucks, five have worn brakes. If eight were randomly picked for inspection, what is the probability that this sample will include three trucks with worn brakes?

This problem can be solved by using the hypergeometric distribution formula. The formula is given by

$$f(x)=\frac{\binom{a}{x}\binom{b}{n-x}}{\binom{a+b}{n}}$$

Solution: To define values, a = the number of successes in the population, x = the number of successes in a sample or what is being asked, b = the failure in the population, and n = sample size.

a = 5; x = 3, 4, 5; b = 11; n = size of the sample

$$f(3)=\frac{\binom{5}{3}\binom{11}{5}}{\binom{16}{8}}$$

f(3) = 0.359

The Excel environment would look like this:

Steps in Excel

1. Open the Excel environment. Click the **fx** button. Choose **HYPGEOMDIST.**
2. Enter **3** in the first window, **8** in the second window, **5** in the third, and **16** in the last.
3. The answer is shown right below the windows.
4. The answer is **0.3589.**

Example 2.19. Given the same information from the previous problem, find the probability that of the eight trucks that were randomly picked for inspection, this sample will include at least how many trucks with worn brakes?

Answer: 0.500

Steps in Excel

1. From the **fx** button, choose **HYPGEOMDIST.**
2. Enter **3** in the first window, **8** in the second window, **5** in the third, and **16** in the last. The answer is shown right below the windows.
3. The answer is **0.3589.**

Since the problem is asking for the probability of at least three worn brakes, then f(4) and f(5) are to be calculated too and added to the f(3) value.

f(3) = **0.359**
f(4) = **0.128**
f(5)= **0.013**
0.359 + 0.128 + 0.013 = 0.500

Example 2.20. A wholesaler has an inventory of one hundred individually boxed whiteboard markers, which he believes to be black, but five are orange. If three of these whiteboard markers are randomly chosen, find the probability that the customer will receive exactly one orange using hypergeometric distribution.

Answer: 0.138

Example 2.21. For a group of twenty PhD engineers, ten are randomly selected for employment. What is the probability that of the ten selected, the five best engineers in the group are included (Wackerly 2008)? Use Excel to calculate the probability.

Answer: 0.016. By performing the same procedure, the computed probability is shown in the picture below.

Example 2.22. A young boy had one blue bag containing five big yellow mangoes and small green mangoes for sale. On his way, he met a group of gang snatchers who took his bag by force. Struggling to keep his mangoes, some of them fell out of the sack. When the police came, the gang ran and the boy was left with only four mangoes. What is the probability that of the four mangoes left, they are all the big yellow mangoes?

Answer: 0.02380

Example 2.23. An industrial company tests its product by samples of five in a lot of twenty items. The guiding benchmark is to reject the lot if there is more than one product that is defective. If the lot contains four defectives, what is the probability that it will be rejected?

Answer: 0.2487. This is calculated by adding $P(Y \geq 2) = P(2) + P(3) + P(4)$.

D. The Normal Distribution

For continuous data like age, height, speed of a car, weight, or the amount of pollution in the air, there exist myriad possibilities, and in many instances, the points of interest are the probabilities associated with intervals, not individual points. For example, one may be interested in finding the probability that at a given time a car is moving between eighty and one hundred kilometres per hour or a particular weight of tuna is more than fifteen kilos and not exactly 10.003 kilograms.

Continuous curves are called probability densities. A probability density is characterized by the following:

> The area under the curve between any two values *a* and *b* gives the probability that a random variable having the continuous distribution will take on a value on the interval from *a* to *b*.

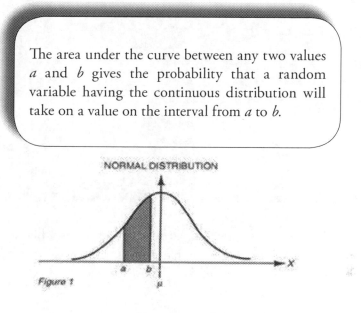

(Answers.com)

Example 2.24. Suppose that a contaminant in samples from a city's water supply has a mean of 500 ppm and a standard deviation of 100 ppm. What is the probability that bacteria in a randomly selected water sample will be A. less than 600 ppm? B. more than 600 ppm? C. between 400 and 600 ppm? (Statistics How To)

Answers

A. 0.841345

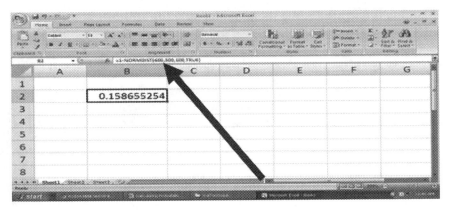

B. Since the area of interest is beyond 600, the area below 600 is deducted from 1 to get its complement. The answer is 0.158655. In Excel, simply edit the formula window by deducting the equation from 1. Refer to the chart below.

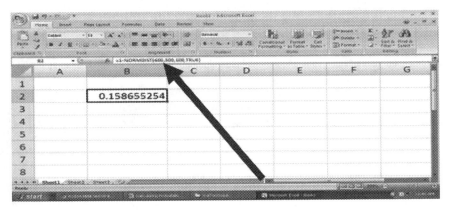

C. To find the area between 400 ppm and 600 ppm, calculate the area at x = 400 by doing the same procedure. Deduct this from the area at x = 600. The answer is 0.68269, found by (0.84134474 − 0.15865526 = 0.68269).

Example 2.25. The weights of sandwich-spread bottles received by a distributor have a mean fill of 220 ml and a standard deviation of 2.3 ml.

A. What percentage of all these sandwich-spread bottles is heavier than 225 ml?
B. What percentage of the sandwich-spread bottles is between 218 and 230 ml?

Answers

A. 0.014856. In Excel, perform = **NORMDIST**(225,220,2.3,**TRUE**). It is going to give you 0.985144167. Note, however, that this is the area to the left of 225 ml. To locate the area heavier than 225 ml is to find the probability to the right of 225 ml. Subtracting 0.985144167 from 1 gives you 0.014856.

B. 0.807724099. Do the = **NORMDIST**(230,220,2.3,**TRUE**) operation. It gives you 0.999993125. Repeat by replacing 230 with 218 = **NORMDIST**(218,220,2.3,**TRUE**). This gives 0.192269026. Subtract the latter from the former. It gives you 0.807724099.

Module 3

Statistical Inference from Quantitative-Qualitative Data

Time-series data represent information about certain magnitudes across years, such as sales, employment rate, inflation, and population. Growth rates and trends can be calculated using these data.

Suppose one wants to learn which labour market, US or UK, is stronger based on unemployment data. The data are the following:

Example 3.1. Unemployment Rates, USA and UK, 1992–2001

Year	USA	UK
1992	7.5	9.7
1993	6.9	10.3
1994	6.1	9.3
1995	5.6	8.0
1996	5.4	7.3
1997	4.9	5.5
1998	4.5	6.5
1999	4.2	5.6
2000	3.9	5.0
2001	3.9	4.1

Before proceeding, one should understand that because raw data could not provide obvious results, the problem set requires some statistical testing. Testing follows a procedure called hypothesis testing, whereby a null hypothesis and alternative hypothesis are presented.

Steps in Hypothesis Testing

1. State the Null Hypothesis (*Ho*). In this example, the null hypothesis is the following:
   Null Hypothesis *Ho:* the average unemployment rate of the USA is equal to the unemployment rate of the United Kingdom.
2. State the Alternative Hypothesis, (*Ha*). In this example, the alternative hypothesis could be stated in one of the three manners.
   a. Alternative Hypothesis *Ha:* On average, the United Kingdom has a higher unemployment rate (one-directional hypothesis statement). Since the *Ha* specifically identifies the United Kingdom as having a higher unemployment rate, the interest is not only on the inequality of two rates between countries but also on the idea that the United Kingdom's rate is higher. This kind of alternative hypothesis is called one tail.
   b. Alternative Hypothesis *Ha:* On average, the United Kingdom has a lower unemployment rate (one-directional hypothesis statement). This is the opposite of a.
   c. Alternative Hypothesis *Ha*: On average, unemployment rates in the United Kingdom and United States are not equal (two-directional hypothesis statement). This test is called two tail, because the directional hypothesis does not favour any specific direction. It could be that the United Kingdom has larger unemployment rates or that it has lower.
3. State the level of significance. In this example, it is set at α: 0.05.
4. Identify the statistical tool that tests the hypothesis. In this example, it is t-test, assuming equal variance.
5. Identify the decision rule concerning accepting or rejecting the null hypothesis or reserving judgments.
6. Make a conclusion on the basis of statistical decisions.

Steps in Excel

1. Enter data, one column for the USA and one column for the United Kingdom.
2. Click **Data,** select **Data Analysis**, choose **t-test: Two-Sample Assuming Equal Variances,** and click **OK.** Then input the required information by highlighting the data one after the other in the **Input Range** window.
3. Try clicking **t-test: Two Sample Assuming Unequal Variances** if there is strong evidence describing the variances or unemployment in the USA and the United Kingdom to be unequal.

Table 3.2 T-Test: Two-Sample Assuming Equal Variances		
	US	UK
Mean	5.29	7.13
Variance	1.563222222	4.58455556
Observations	10	10
Pooled Variance	3.073888889	
Hypothesized Mean Difference	0	
Df	18	
t Stat	–2.34670632	
P(T< = t) one tail	**0.015292558**	
t Critical one tail	1.734063592	
P(T< = t) two tail	**0.030585115**	
t Critical two tail	2.100922037	

Explaining Table 3.2

1. Look at the p value of P(T< = t) one tail. This value is less than the 0.05 level of significance benchmark for acceptance.
2. Since P(T< = t) one-tail value of **0.015292558** is less than the level of significance of 0.05, *Ho* cannot be accepted. Therefore, the null hypothesis *Ho* of no difference in the mean unemployment

rate is rejected. Based on the sample, it appears that the evidence is not strong enough to accept the stated null hypothesis. The alternative hypothesis *Ha* is accepted. Based on the value of the mean, the United Kingdom has a higher unemployment rate, and perhaps one may intuitively say that the United States has a lower unemployment rate and thus is more stable.

3. However, if the *Ha* is nondirectional, *P(T< = t) two tail* will be used as the basis for a decision. Since the value is still less than 0.05, the pool of data does not contain enough evidence to accept the null hypothesis and the alternative of nonequality maybe accepted.

Time as VariableTime as a Variable

Sometimes, the interest is finding the average change of the unemployment rate over time through a specific functional form and the treatment may be different. With t-test, the nonequality of two sets of data has been established, but this does not describe the trend of the rates across time. Such requires a different approach.

Let us revisit the unemployment data in USA and the United Kingdom from 1992 to 2001.

Unemployment Rates, USA and UK, 1992–2001

Year	USA	UK
1992	7.5	9.7
1993	6.9	10.3
1994	6.1	9.3
1995	5.6	8.0
1996	5.4	7.3
1997	4.9	5.5
1998	4.5	6.5
1999	4.2	5.6
2000	3.9	5.0
2001	3.9	4.1

Using the semi-logarithmic approach to times-series data, with a 0.05 level of significance, the results are as follows:

Table 3.3 Regression Table of Unemployment Rates in the United States, 1992-2001, Using Semi-Log Approach

Regression Statistics					
Multiple R	0.99				
R Square	0.98				
Adjusted R Squar	0.98				
Standard Error	0.03				
Observations	10.00				
ANOVA					
	df	SS	MS	F	Significance F
Regression	1.00	0.47	0.47	460.27	0.00
Residual	8.00	0.01	0.00		
Total	9.00	0.48			
	Coefficients	Standard Error	t Stat	P-value	
Intercept	152.87	7.05	21.69	0.00	
Year	-0.08	0.00	-21.45	0.00	

Table 3.4 Regression Table of Unemployment Rates in the United Kingdom, 1992–2001, Using Semi-Log Approach

Multiple R	0.96				
R Square	0.93				
Adjusted R Square	0.92				
Standard Error	0.09				
Observations	10.00				
ANOVA					
	df	SS	MS	F	Significance F
Regression	1.00	0.80	0.80	102.10	0.00
Residual	8.00	0.06	0.01		
Total	9.00	0.86			
	Coefficients	andard Err	t Stat	P-value	
Intercept	198.57	19.46	10.20	0.00	
Year	-0.10	0.01	-10.10	0.00	

Steps in Excel

1. Enter raw data in the columns.
2. In another two columns, calculate the **LN** values of the information corresponding to US and UK data.

2.1 To get the **LN** values, find the *fx* button and click. Choose the **LN** function.

2.2 On the window, click the first information corresponding to the United States; then click **OK**.

2.3 The **LN** value of 7.5 is 2.014903. Click this value, click **Copy**, and then **Paste** it to the cells below it. The whole area will be filled by the **LN** values of the respective raw data for the United States.

2.4 You may extend the pasting to the column next to it and the **LN** values for the United Kingdom will also appear.

3. To establish the regression with respect to time, click **Data**. Click the **Data Analysis** button and choose **Regression**. In the **Input Y Range** window, enter the US data in the **LN** *form* by clicking the entire column corresponding to the US data.

4. On the **Input X Range** window, enter the 'Year' column.

5. Tick **Labels** and **New Worksheet Ply**, and then click **OK**.

Transformed data in the *ln form* are as follows:

Year	lnUS	lnUK
1992	2.014903	2.272126
1993	1.931521	2.332144
1994	1.808289	2.230014
1995	1.722767	2.079442
1996	1.686399	1.987874
1997	1.589235	1.704748
1998	1.504077	1.871802
1999	1.435085	1.722767
2000	1.360977	1.609438
2001	1.360977	1.410987

Corresponding to the year variable in the US table in table 3.1, the coefficient value is −0.075 (or −0.08). The unemployment rate in the United States changes over time at this rate. To identify the value of the intercept, the *ln* value of the first year is taken. That value is around 2.0. Thus, the equation that describes the unemployment rate of the United States with respect to time is given by this:

$$ln \text{ US} = 2.0 - 0.08t$$

This means that the unemployment rate in the United States drops by 8 percent yearly on average. To find the unemployment rate at the beginning of the data sets, the anti-log of 2.0 is taken.

Steps in Excel in Finding the Anti-Log

1. Enter 2.0 in a cell, click the *fx* button, and select **EXP** function.
2. In the window box, enter the cell that contains the value 2.0.
3. Click **OK**. The value registered is 7.5. This is the unemployment rate at the start of the data series, in 1992.

The same procedure is followed using UK data. The coefficient of the variable Year is -0.09849 (or—0.10). Thus, the equation for the UK unemployment rate is given by

$$ln \text{ UK} = 2.27 - 0.10t$$

The equation reads that in the United Kingdom, the unemployment rate dropped by 10 percent every year from 1992 to 2001. The anti-log of 2.27 means that the unemployment rate in 1992 was 9.69.

By comparing the unemployment variations in these economies, it appears that the United Kingdom's unemployment drops faster than that of the United States, making the United Kingdom intuitively more progressive than the United States during those years in consideration.

Example 3.2. Table 3.5 presents the gross domestic product values of Malaysia and the Philippines transformed with February 2013 exchange rates. Check the difference significance and perform the right sequence of hypothesis testing.

Table 3.5. Dollar Value of Gross Domestic Product, Malaysia and the Philippines, 1990–2006, at February 2013 Dollar Exchange Rate, in M$ Constant Price

	Philippines	Malaysia
Year	GDPPhi	GDPMal
1990	17.30	34230.25
1991	17.20	37498.36
1992	17.25	40829.78
1993	17.62	44870.19
1994	18.39	49003.30
1995	19.25	53820.20
1996	20.38	59203.32
1997	21.44	63538.62
1998	21.31	58862.55
1999	22.04	62475.31
2000	23.35	115117.52
2001	23.76	115713.46
2002	24.82	121951.56
2003	26.04	129010.72
2004	27.70	137762.08
2005	29.05	144645.21
2006	30.63	153228.62

Steps in Hypothesis Testing

Ho: The average gross domestic product (GDP) of two countries is the same. (This means that the difference between two values is zero. If it is zero, then the average GDP is equal.)

Ha: The average GDP of two countries is not the same.

Or Ha: The average GDP of Malaysia is greater than that of the Philippines.

$\alpha = 0.05$

Statistical tool: t-test

Steps in Excel

1. Enter data—one column for Philippines data and one column for Malaysia data.
2. Click **Data, Data Analysis, t-Test: Two-Sample Assuming Equal Variances**, **OK**, and then input data by highlighting the data columns one after the other in the **Input Range** window.
3. Try clicking **t-Test: Two Sample Assuming Unequal Variances**.

The results are as follows:

t-Test: Two-Sample Assuming Equal Variances

	GDPPhi	GDPMal
Mean	22.21	83633.00
Variance	18.51	1818588849.24
Observations	17.00	17.00
Pooled Variance	909294433.88	
Hypothesized Mean Difference	0.00	
df	32.00	
t Stat	-8.08	
P(T<=t) one-tail	0.00	
t Critical one-tail	1.69	
P(T<=t) two-tail	0.00	
t Critical two-tail	2.04	

t-Test: Two-Sample Assuming Unequal Variances

	GDPPhi	GDPMal
Mean	22.21	83633.00
Variance	18.51	1818588849.24
Observations	17.00	17.00
Hypothesized Mean Difference	0.00	
df	16.00	
t Stat	-8.08	
P(T<=t) one-tail	0.00	
t Critical one-tail	1.75	
P(T<=t) two-tail	0.00	
t Critical two-tail	2.12	

Explaining Results

1. Assuming equal variance and unequal variance, the null hypothesis cannot be accepted. With a significant p value in both the one-tail and two-tail test, there is enough proof that the difference in GDP values is notably large.
2. Note that prior knowledge about the economic classifications of Malaysia and the Philippines makes one certain about variances. Thus, it is more correct to treat the data using ANOVA assuming unequal variance. There is strong evidence supporting the claim that economic performances of these two economies are not the same. And obviously, it is Malaysia that is growing faster.

Mean Differences of Paired Data

T-test method is limited when samples are not independent. When comparisons are made for usually paired data like the words *before* and *after*, IQs of husbands and wives, performances of male and female mayors in equivalent income levels, etc., a t-test between means shall be that which is prescribed for paired samples. To test the hypothesis that the mean of the first group is equal to the mean of the second group ($\mu 1 - \mu 2 = 0$), we work with the signed difference of *paired data* and test whether this difference may be looked upon as a random sample from a population that has a mean $\mu = 0$.

Example 3.5. The following are the average weekly losses of worker-hours due to accidents in ten industrial plants before and after a certain safety program was put into operation. The management of ten plants knows that accidents are translatable to costs and are factors that reduce a company's profitability and overall market image. So a safety program for the workers is implemented and its impact is assessed. Data are presented in table 3.5.

Table 3.5 Effect on the Safety Program on the Weekly Losses of Worker-Hours due to Accidents (Freund and Williams 1993)

Weekly losses of worker-hours due to accidents before the operation of safety program	Weekly losses of worker-hours due to accidents after the operation of the safety program
45	36
33	35
26	24
73	60
57	51
17	11
46	44
83	77
124	119
34	29

Steps in Hypothesis Testing

1. Ho: $\mu = 0$ (that the difference is zero)
2. Ha: $\mu > 0$ (that the difference is greater than zero, implying more losses have been incurred "before" than "after" the operation of a safety program)
3. Level of significance: 0.05
4. Statistic: t-test for paired data (one-tail test)

Steps in Excel

1. Enter data ("before" in one column "after" data in another column)
2. Click **Data,** select **Data Analysis**, and choose **t-Test (Paired Two Sample for Means)**. Click **OK.**

The results are as follows:

Table 3.6

	Losses before the Operation of Safety Program	Losses after the Operation of Safety Program
Mean	53.8	48.6
Variance	1027.733333	962.9333333
Observations	10	10
Pearson Correlation	0.992175729	
Hypothesized Mean Difference	0	
Df	9	
t Stat	4.033283982	
P(T< = t) one tail	**0.001479161**	
t Critical one tail	1.833112923	
P(T< = t) two tail	0.002958323	
t Critical two tail	2.262157158	

Interpretation

Since the p value for P(T< = t) one tail = 0.001479161 is less than 0.05, the null hypothesis is rejected. There is enough evidence to prove that losses in work-hours due to accidents declined significantly after the implementation of the safety program. The safety program is effective.

Example 3.7. Amounts of copper contents are measured between fresh tomatoes and after these tomatoes have been canned. The objective is to find a significant difference in the copper contents in tomatoes while fresh and after being canned. The data are the following:

Table 3.7 Copper Contents of Fresh Tomatoes and after They Are Canned

											Mean
Fresh tomatoes	0.066	0.079	0.069	0.076	0.071	0.087	0.071	0.073	0.067	0.062	0.0721
Canned tomatoes	0.088	0.088	0.091	0.096	0.093	0.095	0.079	0.078	0.065	0.068	0.0841
										Difference	0.012

Definition: $\mu 1$ is the average copper content of fresh tomatoes.
$\mu 2$ is the average copper content of canned tomatoes.

Steps in Hypothesis Testing

1. Ho: $\mu 1 = \mu 2$ (Mean differences between the copper content of fresh tomatoes and tomatoes after they are canned are zero.)
2. The alternative hypothesis could be stated in two ways, depending on the interest of the study. These may be two-directional or one-directional hypotheses.

Two-directional

a. H1: $\mu 1 \neq \mu 2$
   It says that the mean differences of copper content of fresh tomatoes and tomatoes after they are canned are not equal to zero. This requires a two-tail test.

One-directional
b. H1: $\mu 1 < \mu 2$
    It says that the average copper contents found in fresh tomatoes are less than those in cans. This requires a one-tail test.
3. α: 0.05
4. Statistic: t-test for paired data (two tail)
5. Alternative statistic: t-test for paired data (one tail)

Steps in Excel

1. Click **Data** and then **Data Analysis** in the **Analysis** group. Select **t-Test Paired Two Samples for Means.**

t-Test: Paired Two Sample for Means

	Fresh tomatoes	Canned tomatoes
Mean	0.07	0.08
Variance	0.00	0.00
Observations	10.00	10.00
Pearson Correlation	0.62	
Hypothesized Mean Difference	0.00	
df	9.00	
t Stat	-4.35	
P(T<=t) one-tail	0.00	
t Critical one-tail	1.83	
P(T<=t) two-tail	0.00	
t Critical two-tail	2.26	

Interpretation of Results

1. Since the p values of both tests (one tail and two tail) are less than $\alpha = 0.05$ level of significance, the mean difference is significantly not equal to zero. The null hypothesis could not be accepted.
2. If so, what hypothesis should therefore be accepted? If alternative a) is picked, then the hypothesis that the average copper contents found in fresh tomatoes are larger than those in cans is accepted. If alternative b) is picked, the hypothesis that the average copper contents found in fresh tomatoes is less than those in cans is accepted.

Variances

There are instances when one is interested in finding which among the three or more means of commodities compared vary greatly. The analysis of variance technique is used in this condition.

Example 3.8. The campaign to use generic medicine made one cause-oriented group to study which of the existing paracetamol brands is more effective. The idea is to provide alternatives to buyers by selecting the cheapest paracetamol that is equally effective as the other brands or by buying the most effective, if price differences are insignificant. Effectivity was measured by the number of hours the pill takes effect after administration. The results are as follows:

Table 3.8 Paracetamol Brands and the Average Waiting Time before Effectivity

Bio	Temp	Gen	Cal	Dec
5	9	3	2	7
4	7	5	3	6
8	8	2	4	9
6	6	3	1	4
3	2	7	4	7
$\mu = 5.2$	$\mu = 6.4$	$\mu = 4.0$	$\mu = 2.8$	$\mu = 6.6$

Where Bio is Biocare, Temp is Temperate flu, Gen is Generic, Cal is Calm-oflan, and Dec is Declinogenic.

Hypothesis Testing

1. *Ho*: $\mu = 5.2 = 6.4 = 4.0 = 2.8 = 6.6$
2. *Ha*: at least one is different
3. $\alpha = 0.05$
4. Statistic: *F-test*
5. Decision Rule: Reject Ho if the *p value* is lower than the chosen level of significance. Otherwise, at least one pill is different from the rest.

Steps in Excel

1. Enter data and click **Tools, Data Analysis**.
2. Choose ANOVA **Single Factor**. Check for the *p* value.

Resulting Outcome

Table 3.9 Analysis of Variance Excel Results of Five Paracetamol Brands

Groups	Count	Sum	Average	Variance		
Bio	5.00	26.00	5.20	3.70		
Temp	5.00	32.00	6.40	7.30		
Gen	5.00	20.00	4.00	4.00		
Cal	5.00	14.00	**2.80**	**1.70**		
Dec	5.00	33.00	6.60	3.30		
ANOVA						
Source of Variation	*SS*	*df*	*MS*	*F*	*P-value*	*F crit*
Between Groups	52.00	4.00	13.00	3.25	**0.03**	2.87
Within Groups	80.00	20.00	4.00			
Total	132.00	24.00				

Interpretation

Since the *p* value is less than 0.05, the *Ho* cannot be accepted. This means that the means of the five groups are not the same. From the sample data, brand Cal paracetamol has the lowest average waiting time and variance. It must be the most effective paracetamol drug.

Example 3.9. A study wants to find out if interventions can help stop smoking. One group of smokers (group A) underwent behaviour modifications based on reinforcement theory. The other group (group B) received hypnosis and its complementary mental exercises, and the third group (group C), serving as the control, received no intervention. The dependent variable is cigarette consumption in terms of the number of sticks. Are the various interventions able to affect smoking behaviour? The data are as follows: (Polit and Bernadette 1995)

Table 3.9 Cigarette Consumption of Three Groups

(Polit and Bernadette 1995)

A	B	C
28	22	33
0	31	44
17	26	29
20	30	40
35	34	33
19	37	25
24	0	22
0	19	43
41	24	29
10	27	32

Steps in Excel

1. Enter data, Click **Tools**, **Data Analysis**.
2. Choose ANOVA **Single Factor**. Check for the p value.

Results

Anova: Single Factor

SUMMARY

Groups	Count	Sum	Average	Variance
A	10	194	19.4	183.6
B	10	250	25	106.8888889
C	10	330	33	54.22222222

ANOVA

Source of Variation	SS	df	MS	F	P-value	F crit
Between Groups	934.4	2	467.2	4.066013409	0.028603	3.354131
Within Groups	3102.4	27	114.9037037			
Total	4036.8	29				

Interpretation

Since the *p* value is less than 0.05, the interventions were able to affect smoking behaviour.

Qualitative Data Equality of Proportions

S ome problems require that observed differences are attributable to chance or that the hypothesized proportion is verified by actual experiments.

Example 3.10. A company wants to identify whether the proportion of employees wanting a wage increase is equal to the proportion of employees favouring a benefit improvement. The union expressed that more union members want a salary increase while the above middle management argued that more workers want benefit increase. The administration thinks that differences in proportions of these two groups are not significant.

A. Are the proportions different?
B. How would the administration implement salary increases if some employees prefer salary increases and others favour benefit improvements?

Steps in Hypothesis Testing

1. Null hypothesis: *Ho* = Proportions are the same.
2. Alternative hypothesis: *Ha* = Proportions are not the same.
3. Level of significance: 0.05.
4. Decision rule: If p value is less than 0.05, then *Ho* will be rejected. The *Ha* is accepted.

Table 3.9 Frequency Distribution of Employees Opting for Monetary Compensation and Benefit Increase for Planned Salary Increment, Universal Corporate Agency, 2009 (Hypothetical Data)

Employee Classifications	Mode of salary increment			
		Monetary increase	Benefit increase	totals
Managerial and Executive	(A_1) 93		(B_1) 80	173
Production	(A_2) 65		(B_2) 27	92
Sales Persons	(A_3) 25		(B_3) 35	60
General and Administrative	(A_4) 25		(B_4) 50	75
Totals	208		192	400

Steps in Excel

3. Enter data. Create another table for the observed frequencies.
4. To obtain observed frequencies, follow the formula:
   (Row total * column total)/grand total. For example, to obtain the expected frequencies for *(A1)* = *(173 * 208/400)* = 89.96, for *(A2)* = *(92 * 208)/400* = 47.84, for *(B1)* = *173 * 192/400* = 83.04, etc.
5. The table for completed **expected frequencies** is as follows:

Expected Frequencies	
89.96	83.04
47.84	44.16
31.2	28.8
39	36

These expected frequencies are the proportions of workers in various categories expected to fall in any possible cell. For example, it is expected that thirty-nine from the general and administrative group want monetary increase, but the actual data show that there are only twenty-five *(A4)*. From the same group, thirty-six are expected to opt for a benefit increase, but in actual data, there were 50 *(B4)*. And so on.

6. Once two tables are created, click **fx.**

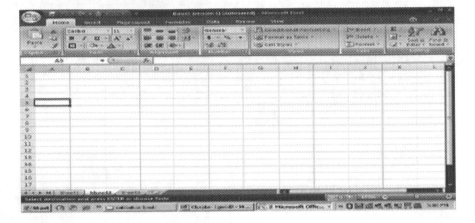

7. Choose **CHITEST.**
8. Highlight the table with actual data and paste it in the corresponding window; then do the same with the expected data.
9. The *p* value is 6.81382E-06. Since this is less than 0.05, the claim that the proportions of employees wanting a monetary increase and benefit increase being equal is rejected. Proportions are different.

Now, this is not the end of the study. Once the hypothesis is verified, the next step is to decide how to proceed. In this example, there were 208 among 400 employees (or 52 percent) opting for a nominal increase and 192 (or 48 percent) opting for benefit increase. What option should prevail?

Three possible actions, depending on the wisdom of the administration, are available. One is majority ruling. Although this is the easiest, the outcome is not progressive all the time. What may be good for many may not be good for the minority, since the choice of the minority is too an expressed preference.

Another option is giving what is preferred. Each employee may fill up a signification form indicating one's option. Those who opt for nominal salary increases will receive monetary raises, and those opting for benefit increases receive what they prefer.

Yet what benefits come in each option? What about the downsides? Salary increments in cash should raise an individual's welfare, but this will also increase the individual's tax payments. On the other hand, salary increments in benefit form are benefit specific. They preclude the enjoyment of other preferable benefits. A retirement benefit, for example, benefits those who are about to retire. Such excludes other desirable benefits like paid vacation. The same condition is applied for insurance or education benefits. Those who self-select not to buy insurance will receive no benefit. Those who decide not to further their education will not take advantage of the education benefit. So long as benefits are not claimed, welfare effect is indeterminate.

Here it is clear that management cost is minimized with benefit increases and employees maximize welfare if benefits are in cash. A conflict is created. To attain what is best for both, negotiation between employees and management or owners is seen as a healthy approach to improved working conditions. A responsible administration always sees what is best for the workforce, and a conscientious worker always delivers his/her best. This has to be translated into high profits for the firms and better working conditions for the labour.

The third possible direction is to increase compensation both in salary and in benefits. The increase in salary may be increased but not as high as expected. If the expected increase is 30 percent without benefits, then the increase could be around 10 to 15 percent and the rest is for the improvement of nonmonetary benefits. In this approach, everybody gets an increase in monetary compensation and everyone is bound to enjoy additional benefits from the company.

Impacts and Effects

There are situations when one is interested in validating what effects variables have to other variables or what association exists between and among variables.

Example 3.10. A travel agency wants to find out if the expenditure on travel has something to do with educational attainment. The objective is to figure out what additional services they can offer to customers. The agency thought that travel and education may be related in some ways.

Table 3.10, which borrowed the data from *Essentials of Econometrics*,[6] has the summary.

Table 3.10 Expenditures on Travel (Y), Income (X), and Education (D)

Tourist's Code Name	Y expenditure on Travel ($, 000)	X Income ($, 000)	High school,D_2=1	College, D_3=1
1	6.0	40	0	1
2	3.9	31	1	0
3	1.8	18	0	0
4	1.9	19	0	0
5	7.2	47	0	1
6	3.3	27	1	0
7	3.1	26	1	0
8	1.7	17	0	0
9	6.4	43	0	1
10	7.9	49	0	1
11	1.5	15	0	0
12	3.1	25	1	0
13	3.6	29	1	0
14	2.0	20	0	0
15	6.2	41	0	1

Does education have anything to do with the amount spent for travel? Income, an established indicator, is included as a factor.

Let us explain the table.

1. Average travel expenditures and incomes are quantitative data. Education data are qualitative data. Why? Education variables require classifications to which each data point falls. The classifications are (to

6   Damodar Gujarati, "Regression on Dummy Explanatory Variables," *Essentials of Econometrics. 2nd ed.* (Singapore: McGraw-Hill Book Co., 1999), 286.

this data set) elementary, high school, and college education levels. If the tourist 's highest educational level is high school, the matrix registers a 1 under the high school column; otherwise, 0. If the tourist's highest educational level is college, the matrix registers a 1 in the college education column; otherwise 0. For tourists 4 and 5, the registered value for high school and college education is 0. Why? It is because tourist 4's and tourist 5's highest educational attainment is the elementary level.

2. A general rule for the dummy variable is that the number of dummies should be one less than the total number of categories. Here, since there are three categories—elementary, high school, and college—the number of dummies is only two.

3. Matrices like this go beyond tabular description. They require statistical treatment. Here the dummy variables "high school" and "college" are qualitative attributes. The values 0 and 1 only represent the presence or absence of a particular attribute. Given data in Table 10, the dependent, variable Expenditures on Travel, a quantitative measure is regressed with Income, a quantitative measure and with Education attributes, a qualitative measure.

4. Because the study requires statistical treatment, relationships and effects are established based on some model.

5. For this data set, the econometric model is

$$Y_i = \beta 1 + \beta 2\ D2i + \beta 3 D3i + \beta 4Xi + \mu i$$

Where

Y_i = annual expenditure on vacation travel

X_i = annual income

$D2$ = 1 if high school education; 0 otherwise

$D3$ = 1 if college; 0 otherwise

μi = stochastic error

6. The hypotheses are

Ho: $\beta 2 = \beta 3 = \beta 4 = 0$

Ha: at least one is not equal to 0

From the equation, the expected mean expenditures are constructed. The expected mean expenditures of the three categories are

For elementary graduates:

$E(Y \mid D2 = 0, D3 = 0, Xi) = \beta 1 + \beta 4Xi.$

This means that if tourists are elementary graduates, meaning they are not high school or college, their information is coded as D2 = 0, D3 = 0,

$Yi = \beta1 + \beta2(0) + \beta3(0) + \beta4Xi + \mu i = \beta1 + \beta4Xi.$

For high school graduates:

$E(Y \mid D2 = 1, D3 = 0, Xi) = (\beta1 + \beta2) + \beta4Xi$ because

$Yi = \beta1 + \beta2(1) + \beta3(0) + \beta4Xi + \mu i = \beta1 + \beta2(1) + \beta4Xi$ or $(\beta1 + \beta2) + \beta4Xi$

For college graduates:

$E(Y \mid D2 = 0, D3 = 1, Xi) = (\beta1 + \beta3) + \beta4Xi$ because

$Yi = \beta1 + \beta2(0) + \beta3(1) + \beta4Xi + \mu i = \beta1 + \beta3 + \beta4Xi$ or $(\beta1 + \beta3) + \beta4Xi$

Steps in Excel

1. Enter data set—one column for each variable.
2. Click on **Data** and choose **Data Analysis**. Sometimes, the data analysis feature is not installed. Have it installed by following instructions from the **Help** button.
3. Under the **Analysis Tools**, choose **Regression.**
4. Click on the **Input Y Range** window and highlight data in the Y column (i.e., the expenditure for travel).
5. Click on the **Input X Range** window. This time, highlight all the remaining variables—income, high school education, and college education.
6. Click the **Labels** and **New Worksheet Ply** buttons.
7. Click **OK**.

Table 3.11a Statistical Output on the Effect of Income, Education to the Average Travel Expenditures

Regression Statistics					
Multiple R	0.998266203				
R Square	0.996535413				
Adjusted R Square	0.995590526				
Standard Error	0.14538542				
Observations	15				
ANOVA					
	df	SS	MS	F	Significance F
Regression	3	66.87682721	22.29227574	1054.660542	8.27968E-14
Residual	11	0.232506122	0.02113692		
Total	14	67.10933333			
	Coefficients	Standard Error	t Stat	P-value	
Intercept	-1.285959184	0.269377693	-4.773814683	0.000577127	✓
X Income ($, 000)	0.172244898	0.014686145	11.72839409	1.4714E-07	✓
High school, D2 =1	0.068	0.170789197	0.398151646	0.698137124	×
College, D3=1	0.447183673	0.395611059	1.130361913	0.282368272	×

Let us explain the output summary in table 3.11.

1. The equation formed is
   Y = –1.285959184 + 0.172244898 X –0.068 HS + 0.447183673 College

2. Based on the usual *t-test*, the p value of income variable is less than the usual 0.05 level of significance; hence, the income coefficient is found significant—and thus is significantly not equal to zero.

3. Its coefficient is 0.172244898, and the sign is positive. This means that for every dollar increase in income, the average travel expenditure *rises* by seventeen cents, other factors constant. The relationship between income and travel spending is positive, and the effect of income to travel is a 0.17 per unit dollar increase.

4. Such a result supports one fundamental assumption of the normality of the demand for leisure, saying that leisure is a normal good. This means that when income rises, the demand for leisure also rises.

5. Now, what is the effect of education to travel spending? If one looks at the p values for D2 and D3, it can be seen that both are greater than 0.05 values. Therefore, the level of education has nothing to do statistically with the variation in travel expenditures, ceteris paribus (having other factors constant).

6. On the other hand, what if the education factor comes out significant? How should one express expectations with mean travel expenditures?

7. To calculate the expected travel spending of elementary graduates, the following is constructed.
   E(Y | D2 = 0, D3 = 0, Xi) = β1 + β4Xi = –1.285959184 + 0.172244898 X
   Thus if If X =Php 18,000, E(Y) =Php 3,099.00; If X = Php19,000, E(Y) = Php3,27.100. This is done by plugging the X value to the equation.

8. For high school graduates, the expected travel spending is given by:
   E(Y | D2 = 1, D3 = 0, Xi) = (β1 + β2) + β4Xi = (–1.285959184 – 0.068) + 0.172244898X
   Or –1.353959184 + 0.172244898 X
   If X = Php31,000; E(Y) = Php 5,338.00

9. The expected travel spending for college graduates is

$E(Y \mid D2 = 0, D3 = 1, Xi) = (\beta1 + \beta3) + \beta4Xi =$
$(-1.285959184 + 0.447183673) +$
$0.172244898\,X$
Or $-0.838775511 + 0.172244898\,X$
If $X = Php\ 40,000$, $E(Y) = Php6,888.00$; If $X = 41,000$, $E(Y)$
$= Php7,061.00$

Table 3.11b Comparing Expected Travel Expenditures with Actual Travel Spending

Expected travel expenditures	Y expenditure on Travel ($, 000)	X Income ($, 000)	High school,D_2=1	College, D_3=1
6.8	6.0	40	0	1
5.3	3.9	31	1	0
3.0	1.8	18	0	0
3.2	1.9	19	0	0
8.0	7.2	47	0	1
4.6	3.3	27	1	0
4.4	3.1	26	1	0
2.9	1.7	17	0	0
7.4	6.4	43	0	1
8.4	7.9	49	0	1
2.6	1.5	15	0	0
4.3	3.1	25	1	0
5.0	3.6	29	1	0
3.4	2.0	20	0	0
7.0	6.2	41	0	1

To show that the education factor is insignificant, Table 3.11b groups similarly situated individuals in education. The data in-between arrows are those with elementary education. The black-shaded part contains those with a high school education. Note that expenditures in both groups are different. The same outcomes are seen in the grey-shaded cells. Therefore, variation in travel spending must come from income variation and not from education.

Now, let us try deleting the income column and regress travel expenditures with education classifications only.

Table 3.12 Summary Output on the Effect of Education to Travel Spending

Y expenditure on Travel ($, 000)	High school, $D_2 = 1$	College, $D_3 = 1$
6.0	0	1
3.9	1	0
1.8	0	0
1.9	0	0
7.2	0	1
3.3	1	0
3.1	1	0
1.7	0	0
6.4	0	1
7.9	0	1
1.5	0	0
3.1	1	0
3.6	1	0
2.0	0	0
6.2	0	1

The summary output is in table 3.13.

Table 3.13 Summary Output on the Effect of Education to Travel Spending

Regression Statistics					
Multiple R	0.97632509				
R Square	0.953218681				
Adjusted R Square	0.945412461				
Standard Error	0.511533642				
Observations	15				
ANOVA					
	df	SS	MS	F	Significance F
Regression	2	63.96933333	31.98467	122.23	1.04925E-08
Residual	12	3.14	0.261667		
Total	14	67.10933333			
	Coefficients	Standard Error	t Stat	P-value	
Intercept	1.78	0.228764799	7.780917	5E-06	✓
High school, D2=1	1.62	0.323522282	5.007383	0.0003	✓
College, D3=1	4.96	0.323522282	15.33125	3E-09	✓

The t-test results show the significance of education to travel spending, with college education having a higher coefficient (4.96). By inspection, the f-test shows model significance as well. Which model now is better: the one in table 3.11 or this one in table 3.13?

One may attempt to show significant results by manipulating data in this manner. The drawback of table 3.13 is that it lacks a strong theoretical grounding. It is direct to connect travel spending with income rather than with education alone without going through the income loop. Education per se does not make travel spending vary but income variations do. The higher the education earned, the higher the salary. Since travel is a normal commodity, travel is stimulated at higher incomes. Hence, income affects more than education does and therefore should be present in the model.

This example only presents the importance of a stable and strong theory, no matter how advanced statistical treatment may be. Nothing replaces a good and sound theoretical background. Methodology simply follows exactly what the theory establishes.

Testing Independence

The chi-square (X^2) test for independence can be used to test the hypothesis of independence of two qualitative variables.

Example 3.14. Suppose one sociologist wants to study the relationship between civil status and the patterns of worship among the residents of one area or community. At random, people are chosen until one thousand respondents have been classified according to faith and whether they worship regularly or not. The data are presented below.

Table 3.14 Patterns of Worship and Civil Status

Patterns of Worship	Civil Status		
	Married	Single	Separated
Worship Regularly	182	213	203
Worship Infrequently	154	138	110

The hypotheses are these:

Ho: Patterns of worship have nothing to do with civil status. (It means that civil status and patterns of prayer are not related.)
Ha: Patterns of worship have something to do with civil status.
Level of significance: 0.05
Statistic: chi-square

Steps in Excel

1. Enter actual data, and then sum the columns and rows.
2. Highlight the first row with data and extend it to the next cell. Click Σ.
3. Do the same to all other columns.
4. Label the empty cell "Total."
5. The grand total is the intersection between the last row and the last column. This value is very critical in the creation of the expected frequency table.

To Create the Expected Frequency Table

1. Click another cell, two or three cells away from the actual frequency table.

2. E = (column total * row total)/grand total.
3. Click "=" in the equation window.
4. Click the first column total. Then go back again to the window and type "*" and click the first row total. Then go back again to the window and type "/" and click the grand total. Press enter.
5. Do the same pattern and fill up all the expected cells.
6. When you are done, click the *fx* button. Click the **CHITEST** function.
7. Excel is going to ask for the range of the actual data. Just highlight the cells with the actual data.
8. Do the same with the expected cells.
9. Before you click **OK**, the computed p value appears on the screen. If there is none, review your work.

Table 3.15

Patterns of Worship	Civil Status			Total
	Married	Single	Separated	
Worship Regularly	182	213	203	598
Worship Infrequently	154	138	110	402
Total	336	351	313	1000
	Expected Table			
	Married	Single	Separated	
	200.928	209.898	187.174	
	135.072	141.102	125.826	
p value	**0.019465613**			

Since the p value is significant, it means that patterns of prayer have something to do with civil status. One sees in the data that more singles worship regularly.

Example 3.16. The Pizza Masa wanted to find out its customers' service satisfaction. Customers are asked to rate each service category. The sample questionnaire is as follows.

Service Category	Excellent	Good	Satisfactory	Unsatisfactory	Total
Food Quality					
Prompt Service					
Cleanliness					
Price Reasonableness					

Server's Name_____

Comments/Suggestions

_____
_____
_____
_____.

What prompted your visit to us?_____
Please drop in suggestions at the entrance. Thank you.

From a sample of 1,200 customers, the summary distribution is presented below. How would the management assess the results?

Table 3.16a.

Service Category	Excellent	Good	Satisfactory	Unsatisfactory	Total
Food Quality	76	87	73	58	294
Prompt Service	84	67	65	76	292
Cleanliness	81	79	74	64	298
Price Reasonableness	89	85	87	55	316
Total	330	318	299	253	1200

Table 3.16 b.Expected Frequency Table

Expected Frequency					
Food Quality	80.85	77.91	73.26	61.99	
Prompt Service	80.30	77.38	72.76	61.56	
Cleanliness	81.95	78.97	74.25	62.83	p value 0.32
Price Reasonableness	86.90	83.74	78.74	66.62	

Possible interpretation

By inspection, the management could think they are rated highest in the price reasonableness (316 highest frequency) criterion and on average are rated "excellent" overall (330 the highest frequency too). However, are these conclusions by the management statistically sound?

The chi-test for significance for proportion below reveals that the differences in proportions of customers across categories are not large enough. (P value is greater than 0.05.) It means that the proportion of customers rating "excellent" is the same with the proportions of customers giving lower ratings, implying that the market considers the pizza restaurant a so-so eatery.

To conclude, Pizza Maza has yet to attain its dominance and leadership in the industry it operates and the market it serves.

Constant Elasticities

Nonlinear results in parameters may be transformed functionally to make parameters linear. Once transformed, the numerical coefficients will be interpreted as the percentage changes effects. Consider the percentage change in GDP in Mexico as a consequence of a percentage change in labour inputs and capital stock. This model is called the constant elasticity model.

Table 3.17 Gross Domestic Product, Labour Employment, Fixed Capital Stock, Mexico, 1955–1974 (Gujarati 1999)

GDP Millions of 1960 Pesos	Employment in Thousands of People	Fixed Capital in Millions of 1960 Pesos
114043	8310	182113
120410	8529	193749
129187	8738	205192
134705	8952	215130
139960	9171	225021
150511	9569	237026
157897	9527	248897
165286	9662	260661
178491	10334	275466
199457	10981	295378
212323	11746	315715
226977	11521	337642
241194	11540	363599
260881	12066	391847
277498	12297	422382
296530	12955	455049
306712	13338	484677
329030	13738	520553
354057	15924	561553
374977	14154	609825

The questions are the following:

1. What significant relationships do labour input and capital stock have with gross domestic product?
2. How much percentage change has there been observed for every percentage change in labour input having the capital stock unchanged?

3. How much percentage change has there been observed for every percentage change in capital stock having labour employment unchanged?
4. Which of the factors explains significantly the changes made in gross domestic product?

Hypotheses Testing

1. Ho: Labour and capital inputs do not significantly affect the movements of GDP.
2. Ha: At least one of the inputs affects significantly the movements of GDP.
3. Level of significance: 0.05.
4. Statistical tool: regression.

Functional Transformation

1. The raw data will be transformed by finding the natural log of the values. The transformed data are in the table that follows:

Table 3.18 Transformed Data in Table 3.17 in Log Values

Year	GDP millions of 1960 Pesos	Employment in thousands of people	Fixed Capital in millions of 1960 pesos
1955	11.64433085	9.025214888	12.11238265
1956	11.69865786	9.0512274	12.17431879
1957	11.76901625	9.07543661	12.23170141
1958	11.81084248	9.09963225	12.27899778
1959	11.84911195	9.123801611	12.32394901
1960	11.92179145	9.166283986	12.37592512
1961	11.9696982	9.161885152	12.42479444
1962	12.01543259	9.175955945	12.47097599
1963	12.09229346	9.243194709	12.52621949
1964	12.20335395	9.303921786	12.59601117
1965	12.26586398	9.371268036	12.66259519

1966	12.33260397	9.351926736	12.72974144
1967	12.39335687	9.35357454	12.80380689
1968	12.47181964	9.398146859	12.87862674
1969	12.533569	9.417110609	12.9536654
1970	12.59990367	9.469237093	13.02816038
1971	12.63366448	9.498372383	13.09123797
1972	12.70390421	9.527920995	13.16264699
1973	12.7772132	9.675582684	13.23846144
1974	12.83461997	9.557752549	13.32092731

2. The transformed data will be treated using the ordinary least squares method.

Steps in Excel

1. Enter the data in columns—GDP, Labour Input, and Capital Stock. Make another same number of columns for the natural log values.
2. Click on an empty cell under the GDP. Click the *fx* button and locate the **LN** function.
3. On the window, highlight the first raw value of GDP.
4. Copy the first cell and paste it to the rest of the data. Do the same to labour and capital-stock data set.
5. To solve for regression, click **Data** and **Data Analysis** in the analysis group and select **Regression**. Click **OK**. On the **Input Y Range**, highlight the GDP log values. On the **Input X Range**, highlight the columns with the log of labour and log of capital.
6. Check **Labels** and **New Worksheet Ply.** Click **OK.**

The results are the following:

Table 3.19	Gross Domestic Product, Labor Input, Capital Stock, 1955-1974				
Regression Statistics					
Multiple R	0.9975586				
R Square	0.995079				
Adjusted R Square	0.9945				
Standard Error	0.028293				
Observations	20				
ANOVA					
	df	SS	MS	F	Significance F
Regression	2	2.751646	1.375823	1718.75	2.41291E-20
Residual	17	0.013608	0.0008		
Total	19	2.765254			
	Coefficients	Standard Error	t Stat	P-value	
Intercept	-1.65207	0.606328	-2.72471	0.014411	
Employment in thousands of people	0.339649	0.185732	1.828702	0.085044	
Fixed Capital in millions of 1960 pesos	0.846031	0.093871	9.060965	6.44E-08	

Interpretation of Results

1. The elasticity of output with respect to labour input is 0.339649. This means that for a 1 percent increase in labour input, output on average goes up by 0.339649 percent, having capital input the same.
2. Similarly, holding labour input the same, a percentage increase in capital input raises output on average by about 0.846031 percent.
3. The signs of coefficients are both positive, implying the positive relationship between inputs and the output.
4. Adding the elasticities generates another important parameter in economics: the returns to scale parameter. If elasticities **add up to 1**, the returns to output are called *constant returns to scale*. If it is **greater than 1**, the returns to output are called *increasing returns to scale,* and if it is **less than 1**, the returns to output are called *declining returns to scale*. In this example, since 0.846031 + 0.339649 = 1.185679 and is greater than 1, then it can be described that the growth of the Mexican economy during the period suggests an increasing return to scale. This means that the output on the average increases by more than the proportionate change in inputs.
5. R^2 = 0.995079 states that 99 percent of the variations in the log of GDP are explained by the variations in the log of labour employment and capital stock.
6. Since the estimated value of **F** is very small, then it can be said that the combined impact of labour and capital to GDP is significant.

7. The inputs are statistically significant at a one-tail test with capital impact as generating a larger effect. (Divide the p value of labour and capital by 2 and the corresponding result is compared with 0.05.)

Growth Functions

Oftentimes, growth-rate information (for instance, on consumer credit outstanding or growth of output) is necessary to monitor effectiveness of certain policies. Semi-log models are used for this type of function.

Example 3.18. An interested office wants to measure the consumer credit outstanding of the United States from 1973 to 1987. The data are as follows:

Table 3.20 Consumer Credit Outstanding, Values in Log, US, 1973–1987 (Gujarati 1999)

Years	Consumer Credit Outstanding	Consumer Credit Outstanding (in log)
1973	190601	12.15793752
1974	199365	12.20289259
1975	204963	12.23058475
1976	228162	12.33781118
1977	260808	12.47153978
1978	308072	12.6380888
1979	347507	12.75854009
1980	349386	12.76393261
1981	366597	12.81201843
1982	381115	12.85085645
1983	430382	12.97242847
1984	511768	13.14562668
1985	592409	13.29195255
1986	646055	13.37863992
1987	685545	13.43796942

Steps in Excel

1. Enter data in two columns—year and consumer credit outstanding.
2. On the third column, calculate the natural log *ln* by finding the *ln* function with the **fx** button.
3. When values have already been logged, click the **Data** button.
4. Click **Data Analysis** and choose **Regression**.
5. Enter the consumer credit outstanding in log values to the window bar asking for **Y range,** by highlighting the column with the data. For **X range,** enter the year column.
6. Click **OK.** The results are as follows:

Table 3.21 Excel Output on the Semi-Log Treatment on Values on Table 3.20

Multiple R	0.9912				
R Square	0.982478				
Adjusted R Square	0.98113				
Standard Error	0.058735				
Observations	15				
ANOVA					
	df	SS	MS	F	Significance F
Regression	1	2.514568035	2.514568	728.9119	8.38088E-13
Residual	13	0.044846823	0.00345		
Total	14	2.559414858			
	Coefficients	Standard Error	t Stat	P value	
Intercept	–174.873	6.949945123	–25.1618	2.06E-12	
Years	0.094766	0.003510065	26.99837	8.38E-13	

Explaining Table 3.21

1. The consumer credit outstanding is found to grow instantaneously by 9.4 percent per year. This is the coefficient the of "Years" variable.

2. Such a trend is significant at 5 percent level of significance. This is verified by the small value of the p value.

   The equation therefore constructed is

   Y(consumer credit outstanding) = 12.15793752 + 0.094766 Years

   (0.00000)   (0.0000)

3. By getting the anti-log of 12.15793752, we have 190,601. The consumer credit outstanding in 1973 is 190,601.

Module 4

Making Decisions from Statistical Information

S tatistical information is the root for decision-making, and for this matter, sufficient and appropriate data is required to afford stable and more precise action. For various decisions made every day, statistical quality control is one vital aspect the manager should pay attention to.

Statistical quality control is a specialized technique practically used to reduce variability in production. The final objective of this system is to increase profits by producing products of exactly the same quality across production volumes. During this process, characteristics of the products are observed, assessed, and compared with some type of standard. This involves considerable use of sampling procedures and statistical measures.

Control Charts

F or the most part of statistical quality control, decision-making concerning production quality is made based on statistical sampling techniques. It is believed that fundamental to all production is that there is no such thing as two identical parts (Mason 1974). Thus given a more precise measuring instrument, any difference should be discernible.

The purpose of a control chart is to determine if the performance of a process is maintaining an acceptable level of quality (Walpole and Myers 1993). It is intended to detect the nonrandom or the out-of-control condition of the process. What is expected is that possible variation that would occur is natural and within acceptable levels defined in the standards. Any deviation outside the standardized boundaries signals a possible machinery check or machinery replacements.

Bar charts ($\bar{X}$), also called mean charts, are designed to portray variation in the process system. For this to work, it is essential to identify the process average and standard deviation. If the actual mean and standard deviation are known, then these figures will be used. However, in actual practical scenarios, population mean (μ) and standard deviation (δ) are not known. In situations like these, sample mean and sample standard deviation may be used.

Example 4.1. To determine the average weights of glass containers produced, a sample of five was taken every thirty minutes during the production process and data are arranged in the table below.

Table 4.1 Weights of Five Glass Containers Selected at Random Every Half Hour

	Weights of Sample Number						
Time	1	2	3	4	5	Sum	Mean
8:00A.M.	30	31	30	30	31	152	30.4
8:30 A.M.	29	30	28	29	30	146	29.2
9:00 A,M,	31	30	29	30	31	151	30.2
9:30 A.M.	32	28	30	30	30	150	30.0
							119.8

$\bar{X}$ or μ = 29.95 [found by 119.8/4]

The population mean (μ) and standard deviation (δ) are not known. Thus, to establish the limits, sample mean and standard deviation values are utilized. This represents the μ, and given this result, the $\bar{X}$ acceptable weights should be within

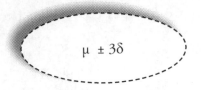

$$\mu \pm 3\delta$$

The standard deviation (s.d.) is required to calculate the upper and lower boundaries where values in between are acceptable. The s.d. value is **0.52599113.** This means that weights within acceptable limits are those from **28.37203** to **31.52797.** Values less than **28.37203** (or the lower control limit [LCL]) and greater than **31.52797** (the upper control limit [UCL]) are information of production concerns. The graphical picture is shown in chart 4.1.

Chart 4.1 Production Trend within Upper Control Limit and Lower Control Limit

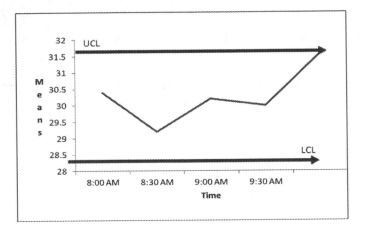

*Values outside the bold lines may indicate serious production concerns.

In some cases, the limits are defined using this formula:

$$\mu \pm \frac{\delta}{\sqrt{n}}$$

where μ is the mean,
δ is the standard deviation, and
n is the sample size.

Steps in Excel

1. Enter data. In the next cell of the first row, click the **fx** button.
2. Choose **Average.** Highlight the values in the first row. Click **OK.**
3. The answer registered must be 30.4.
4. To do the same for the other rows, simply click the cell with **30.4**.
5. Click **Copy,** and drag to the cells you need to copy the operation. Click **Paste**.
6. The values **29.2**, **30.2**, and **30** should appear in exact orientation as the given data.
7. To find the average of the averages, click another empty cell below the average columns. Click **fx** again, and highlight the column data in the average portion.
8. Click **OK**. The value **29.95** should appear.
9. To find the standard deviation, click again the **fx** button and select **STDEV**.
10. Highlight the values registered in step 8.
11. Click **OK**. The value coming out is **0.52599113**. This is the standard deviation

Sometimes, it is convenient to estimate standard deviation from the information related to the ranges in the samples rather than standard deviation. An **R chart** uses the range as the determining factor for control limits. A **range** is calculated by getting the difference between the highest and lowest values in the set. In the previous example, the range in the first row is 1, the second row is 2, the third row is 3, and the last row is 4. The average of these ranges is **2.25**. This average range is multiplied with some constant **As**, the values of which are found in **table 4.2.**

Table 4.2 Factors for Control Charts

Number of items in samples	Chart for averages	Chart for Ranges		
	Factors for control limits	Factors for central line	Factors of Control limits	
N	A_s	D_2	D_3	D_4
2	1.880	1.228	0	3.267
3	1.023	1.693	0	2.575
4	0.729	2.059	0	2.282
5	0.577	2.326	0	2.115
6	0.483	2.534	0	2.004
7	0.419	2.704	0.076	1.924
8	0.373	2.847	0.136	1.864
9	0.337	2.970	0.184	1.816
10	0.308	3.078	0.223	1.777
11	0.285	3.173	0.256	1.744
12	0.266	3.258	0.284	1.716
13	0.249	3.336	0.308	1.692
14	0.235	3.407	0.329	1.671
15	0.223	3.472	0.348	1.652

Going back to the earlier example, with a sample size of 5, the corresponding **As** value presented from the table is 0.577. Using this figure, the estimated limits are calculated using the following formula:

$$\mu \pm A_s * R_{ave}$$

where μ is the sample mean $\bar{x}$,
A_s is the tabular value factors for control limits, and
R_{ave} is the average range.

Therefore, the control limits are **28.65 – 31.25** found by 29.95 ± 0.577(2.25).

Especially when variation is too wide, the use of R_{ave} could be more beneficial. UCL and UCL are calculated using the D3 and D4 values. (Refer to table 2.) In the example earlier, **UCL = D4 * R_{ave}** (2.115 * 2.25) and **LCL = D3 * R_{ave}** (0 * 2.25) and the limits are **4.754875** and **0**. This means that the variation of each glass should not be larger than **4.754875** to stay within acceptable levels.

A *p chart* ($\bar{p}$) is specifically used in controlling the number of defectives in a production process. This is also called the fraction defective chart. The chart portrays the percentage of production that is not acceptable.

Example 4.2. Suppose that a roll of steel exactly two hundred inches long and one inch wide is fed into an automatic machine that cuts off a one-inch piece and at the same time punches a hole in the centre of the piece. The two hundred square pieces are then moved to the assembly line. If for any reason a piece cannot be used, the worker puts it aside. The record of the first five production runs is as follows (Mason 1974):

Table 4.3 Steel Production (Number, Number of Defectives, and Percent of Defectives)

Production Number	Number of pieces produced	Number of pieces defective	Percent defective (%)
1	200	4	0.02
2	200	3	0.015
3	200	5	0.025
4	200	6	0.03
5	200	2	0.01
		Σ % defectives = 0.01	

The average defective ($\bar{p}$) is Σ percent defectives divided by number of sample groups. This is equal to 0.02 found by (0.01/5 = 0.02). The UCL and LCL are calculated using the following formula:

$$\bar{p} \pm 3\,\delta$$

where $\delta = \sqrt{\dfrac{p(1-p)}{n}}$

Hence, given the data above, the limits are

$$\text{UCL} = 0.02 + \sqrt{\frac{0.02(0.98)}{200}}\,3$$

$$= 0.0497$$

LCL = 0 should be 0

Example 4.3. The US administration was interested in how fluctuations of labour and capital inputs have been influencing the country's economic performance. Given the data below, calculate the upper and lower limit of the production index measured in the GDP index.

a. What opinion can be expressed on the computed results?
b. Do the same to calculate the UCL and LCL of the labour input. Make observations about the variables. What opinion about labour input can be assumed about the results?

Table 4.4 Output, Labour Input, and Capital Input, United States, 1957-1967 (Maddala 2001)

Year	Output	Labor Input	Capital Input
1957	422.8	56809	1255.5
1958	418.4	55023	1287.9
1959	445.7	56215	1305.8
1960	457.3	56743	1341.4
1961	466.3	56211	1373.9
1962	495.3	57078	1399.1
1963	515.5	57540	1436.7
1964	544.1	58508	1477.8
1965	579.2	60055	1524.4
1966	615.6	62130	1582.2
1967	631.1	63162	1645.3

*This data set is only an excerpt of a longer data series where

- output is the index of gross national product in constant dollars,
- labour input is the total number of persons engaged in labour activity, and
- capital input is the capital stock in constant dollars.

Answer: $\mu \pm 3\delta = 508.3 \pm (3 * 75.36)$

a. The limits are **282.21 – 734.39.**

b. Possible opinion

Production is observed to fluctuate within the expected ranges. If production goes beyond the expected range, some unanticipated interplay of extraneous variables must have significantly affected the growth of domestic production. These might include, but are not limited to, the unprecedented increased or declined political confidence or social assurance from the international community—or any other factors expected to significantly affect aggregate production.

c. The limits are **50,351.55-65,916.45.** One approach to make an opinion about the data set is to graph the data points and generate an idea coming from the figure formed. The graph may look like the following:

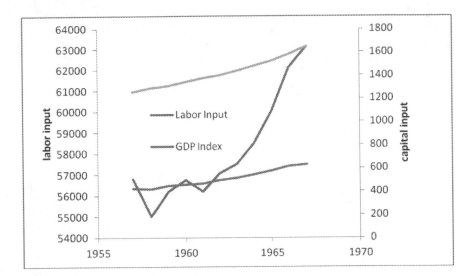

Hypothetically, domestic production positively relates with capital stock. Though labour input varies erratically and slopes steeply, the GDP curve slopes flatly and moves in a similar fashion with that of the capital index line. This may suggest that capital stock is one significant factor essential in inducing GDP to fluctuate highly. Comparing labour and capital effects, the graph suggests inelasticity of economic growth with respect to the labour input employed.

Example 4.4. Calculate the same data for limits using this equation: $\mu \pm \delta/n^{1/2}$.

Answer

GDP limit: 484.47 – 532.13
Capital stock limit: 57,313.65 – 58,954.34
Labour input: 1,381.18 – 1,460.64

Steps in Excel Concerning Power

1. Click the *fx* button.
2. Choose **Power.**
3. In the new template that opens, enter the base number you raise in power. In this example, it is 10.
4. In the next window, enter the desired power. In this example, it is ½ or the inverse of square root.
5. Click **OK.**

Steps in Excel on Creating Charts

1. Enter data in table form.
2. Highlight the tabulated data.
3. Click **Insert** and choose **Scatter** in the **Chart** category.
4. From among the scatter options, try each style in a trial-and-error approach to see the resulting outcome of each trial. Click **OK** once satisfied with the final option selected.
5. The chart formed is raw and void of a genuine and understandable pattern. There is a need to further reformat the chart. Click **Format.**
6. Click on the **Labour Input Series** line in the chart area.
7. On the **Current Selection** window below the **Home** button, click **Format Selection.** Refer to the picture below. This means that the labour input series shall undergo a chart reformatting.
8. A **Format Data Series** window will open. Select **Primary Axis.**
9. Repeat the same steps to format the **Capital Input Series.** This time, choose **Secondary Axis.**
10. Then repeat the procedure to format the **Output Series** and choose the **Secondary Axis.**
11. Improve the chart by exploring all of its capabilities via trial and error.
12. The resulting Excel environment looks like the following:

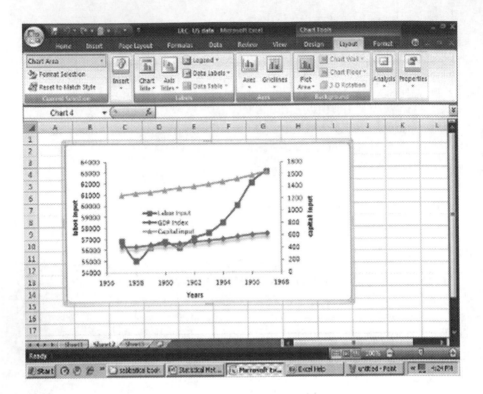

Example 4.5. Consider the example in Table 4.4. Identify the UCL of thirty lots with one hundred samples per lot (Freund, Williams, and Pearles 1993). How many lots fail to meet the standards, and what must be done with them? Recalculate the UCL after eliminating the lots that fail to meet the standards.

Lot Number	sample size	Number of defectives	fraction defectives
1	100	5	0.05
2	100	2	0.02
3	100	4	0.04
4	100	6	0.06
5	100	3	0.03
6	100	2	0.02
7	100	0	0
8	100	9	0.09
9	100	15	0.15
10	100	3	0.03
11	100	2	0.02
12	100	2	0.02
13	100	0	0
14	100	6	0.06
15	100	3	0.03
16	100	4	0.04
17	100	2	0.02
18	100	0	0
19	100	5	0.05
20	100	4	0.04
21	100	2	0.02
22	100	1	0.01
23	100	1	0.01
24	100	2	0.02
25	100	1	0.01
26	100	0	0
27	100	1	0.01
28	100	2	0.02
29	100	2	0.02
30	100	1	0.01

Solution

$$\bar{p} \pm 3\,\delta$$

where $\delta = \sqrt{\dfrac{p(1-p)}{n}}$

$$0.03 + 3\sqrt{\dfrac{0.03(0.97)}{100}}$$

UCL = 0.081
LCL must be zero.

The acceptable proportion of defectives must be ≤ **0.081**. This means that the number of defectives should be at most eight per one hundred units.

Answer: Two lots produced more than eight defectives. These are lot numbers 8 and 9. This means these two lots are out of control and machines may be checked for efficiency. Once defectives are identified, these are eliminated from the production stream.

Lot Number	sample size	Number of defectives	fraction defectives
1	100	5	0.05
2	100	2	0.02
3	100	4	0.04
4	100	6	0.06
5	100	3	0.03
6	100	2	0.02
7	100	0	0
8	100	3	0.03
9	100	2	0.02
10	100	2	0.02
11	100	0	0
12	100	6	0.06
13	100	3	0.03
14	100	4	0.04
15	100	2	0.02
16	100	0	0
17	100	5	0.05
18	100	4	0.04
19	100	2	0.02
20	100	1	0.01
21	100	1	0.01
22	100	2	0.02
23	100	1	0.01
24	100	0	0
25	100	1	0.01
26	100	2	0.02
27	100	2	0.02
28	100	1	0.01

After eliminating lots 8 and 9, the UCL limit becomes

$$0.023 + 3\sqrt{\frac{0.023(0.977)}{100}}$$

$$= 0.0679$$

The upper control limit is reduced to 0.0679. The standard has improved and the limits have been narrowed to 0.0679. With this new information, the production defectives in proportion to the total identified sample size should not be more than seven units per one hundred.

Example 4.6. The following is the control chart of loose frying-pan handles produced by a kitchenware manufacturer (Freund and William 1993).

Table 4.5. Lot Number, Sample Size, Number of Defectives of Loose Frying Pan Handles

Lot Number	Sample Size	Number of defectives
1	200	9
2	200	8
3	200	6
4	200	6
5	200	4
6	200	7
7	200	10
8	200	9
9	200	8
10	200	5
11	200	8
12	200	16
13	200	5
14	200	12
15	200	8
16	200	9
17	200	8
18	200	7
19	200	9
20	200	13
21	200	4
22	200	6
23	200	9
24	200	7
25	200	7

Calculate the proportion of defectives; determine the centre line and the control limits for fraction defectives. Plot the twenty-five subgroups, and present your observations.

Answer

Lot Number	Sample Size	Number of defectives	fraction defectives
1	200	9	0.045
2	200	8	0.040
3	200	6	0.030
4	200	6	0.030
5	200	4	0.020
6	200	7	0.035
7	200	10	0.050
8	200	9	0.045
9	200	8	0.040
10	200	5	0.025
11	200	8	0.040
12	200	16	0.080
13	200	5	0.025
14	200	12	0.060
15	200	8	0.040
16	200	9	0.045
17	200	8	0.040
18	200	7	0.035
19	200	9	0.045
20	200	13	0.065
21	200	4	0.020
22	200	6	0.030
23	200	9	0.045
24	200	7	0.035
25	200	7	0.035

The average defective proportion is **0.04** (or 4 percent). The number of defectives should not be greater than **8.1 percent. (0.081).**

Answer

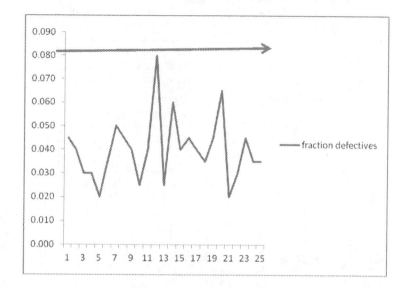

Comment: Overall, the machines are operating efficiently, producing defectives within the control limit. However, special attention may be given to lot number 12. It has the highest number of loose frying-pan handles.

Example 4.7. At Western Visayas College of Science and Technology (WVCST), in the Philippines, the administration plans to implement a punctuality-enhancement policy by awarding faculty who are reported to be prompt and dedicated in the teaching profession. In the past, it has been observed that teachers who habitually come to class late or are absent are those with special assignments—administrative or academic. In this regard, the administration wants to find the centre line of "minutes late of faculty" to make the policy proposal more data based. The results are the following:

Sample No.	College A	College B	College C	College D	Faculty with special projects and administrative assignments
					Minutes
1	11	15	10	30	28
2	12	0	8	30	20
3	20	10	20	15	30
4	11	5	18	25	7
5	10	18	7	8	20
6	15	0	25	30	10
7	1	5	5	28	25
8	15	5	30	20	10
9	30	5	8	6	5
10	7	4	10	10	30
11	18	18	25	15	20
12	1	5	30	8	18
13	25	3	20	12	8
14	30	5	28	30	8
15	30	12	15	7	20
16	30	18	30	20	0
17	6	5	10	30	30
18	18	25	6	30	18
19	12	30	5	28	30
20	13	10	20	7	12
21	15	18	28	3	14
22	11	13	20	4	18
23	10	30	7	15	7
24	18	12	25	10	27
Averages	15.38	11.29	17.08	17.54	17.29

Given the sample results, compute for the overall centre line and the upper and lower control limits of faculty's lateness in minutes following the $\mu \pm 3\delta$ formula.

Using the same data, calculate the UCL and LCL using $\mu \pm \delta/n^{1/2}$.

- Is the observation true that those with special assignments come to class late more often than the regular faculty do? Interpret the results.

Use the same data to calculate the limits using ranges.

- What suggestions could be made to curb teachers' tardiness?

Answers

a. $\bar{\bar{X}} = 15.72$ $\delta = 2.62$

The centre line is 15.72 minutes, and the minutes-late limits are 7.86 and 23.58 minutes. This means that, on average, the acceptable minutes late of faculty, as a whole, is within **7.86** and **23.58** minutes.

b. $15.72 \pm 2.62/(120)^{1/2}$. The limits are **15.480 – 15.96.**
c.   There is not enough strength in the observation that faculty with special assignments come late compared to ordinary faculty. From the data, teachers from colleges C and D also come late at similar minute rates.
d. $\mu \pm As * R_{ave}$
$R_{ave} = 28.8$
$\mu = 15.72$

With twenty-four samples in a group, the table is not extensive enough to provide values for more than 15. Hence, the figure on the fifteenth sample may be taken.

$As = 0.223$ (for fifteen samples)

Hence, the limits are **9.30 – 22.14.** This means that, on average, the sample faculty comes to class late at least **9.30 minutes** and at **most 22.14 minutes**.

Using ranges, the variance becomes larger. This could allow faculty more time in moving from one classroom to another and from one building to another within the university. However, for an hour-long class, this maximum tolerance level creates a significant amount of inefficiencies in teaching and classroom learning. A stricter time allowance induces more creative classroom activity. The maximum late time allowed may be set at fifteen minutes at the most.

e.   Further investigations may be implemented. Those coming beyond the allowable limits may have legitimate reasons. Reasons possibly include health conditions, age, administrative responsibilities, etc.

If lateness is caused by some health-related grounds like recuperating from a minor operation or suffering from insomnia, the suggestion is to rearrange classroom and schedule assignments, giving consideration to the faculty.

If the cause is advancement in age, the administration may rearrange schedules of faculty, giving the older faculty the preferred midday schedules. However, if reasons are connected to administrative assignments, the system may design a co-worker in each assignment—say assistant director, associate vice president, junior dean, co-adviser, sub-president, etc.—specific assignments which may be clearly defined having an objective of not trading off administrative efficiency with the sanctity of the teaching profession.

There is another way of possibly curbing tardiness. This is by giving incentives to individuals who have never been late. It could be in the form of a scheme of rewards consisting of promotion units, vacation bonus, recognition awards, plaques of appreciation, or in any kind or form to the choice of the faculty concerned.

While giving reprimand is an outright managerial approach many heads take, such has been found counterproductive and weak in addressing the issue. On the other hand, a more constructive method of handling human beings, by empowering instinctive choice preferences and rewarding those that support the higher objectives of the school rather than punishing undesirable action, is found more valuable and gratifying. But truly, such admirable quality requires both a profound humanitarian outlook and an excellent problem-solving IQ of the school administrator. Absence of these may even exacerbate inefficiency problems endured by the school.

Opportunity Costs

There are situations when the factor that matters a lot in doing certain actions is the cost generated. If it is possible for decisions to be made based on what benefits can be derived out of doing the action, there are also decisions that are made on the basis on which action is least costly to do.

Example 4.8

A contractor received a two-option offer. He will be paid a monthly salary of $10,000 for six months for construction work on a ten-storey building or a straight fee of double the salary, given only when the work is finished. If, however, the project is uncompleted after six months, all payments due will be source.

   a. Construct a loss-decision tree for the contractor.
   b. What do you think is the best (most desirable) option? Construction specifications are assumed met and budget for other factor inputs is available.

Loss-Decision Tree for the Contractor

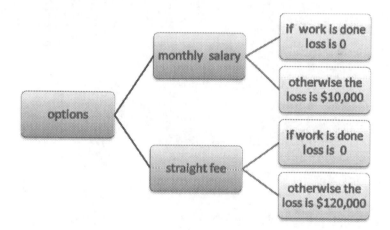

If the monthly mode is chosen, the maximum amount forfeited is $10,000. However, if the straight fee is chosen, the maximum loss is $120,000. The magnitude of loss would be one thousand times over. The better outcome is having a lower potential loss of $10,000. Therefore, the better option is the monthly salary.

On the other hand, from the point of the client, if he believes in the contractor's capability—his speed and accuracy—he would not hesitate to offer the double-pay reward. However, if he thinks the contractor needs more experience on big projects, he has the hunch that the contractor is likely to choose the monthly mode of payment. If the contractor opts for the straight fee but is a neophyte on this job, the client loses nothing. Instead, he gains the unfinished work left by the contractor.

Another manner of making decisions is to present outcomes in terms of costs in a loss table.

Example 4.9. Suppose a family is deciding which TV brand to buy. The following table shows the various prices TV dealers are giving.

    a.   Compute for the opportunity loss.
    b.   Create an opportunity-loss table.

Table 4.9 TV Sets and the Price Offers of Three Dealers

	Dealer 1	Dealer 2	Dealer 3
TV Set A	2,850	2,530	2,500
TV Set B	3,450	3,520	3,600

Solution: Find the cheapest value in each row and deduct it from each value in other cells. The opportunity loss is

2,850 – 2,500 = **350**; 2,530 – 2,500 = **30**; 2,500 – 2,500 = **0**
3,450 – 3,450 = **0**; 3,520 – 3,450 = **70**; 3,600 – 3,450 = **150**

Opportunity-Loss Table

	Dealer 1	Dealer 2	Dealer 3
TV Set A	350	30	0
TV Set B	0	70	150

Since there are zeros in each row, then the minimum criterion (minimizing loss) could not lead to a unique course of action. However, an alternative criterion minimax (minimizing maximum loss) can be used. Back to the table, the smallest loss among the three dealers is dealer 2. (A maximum loss of 70 is better than a loss of 350 or 150.) The family may now visit dealer 2.

Example 4.10. Given table 4.10, kindly identify what the manager must choose from regarding expanding the business now and delaying it.

Table 4.10 Payoff Table on Options to Expand Now or Delay Expansion, Given Mutually Exclusive Economic Conditions

Economic conditions are good	$369,000	$180,000
There is a recession	-$90,000	$18,000

Solution

1.   Subtract the lower value from the larger value in each row.

First Row: 369,000 – 180,000 = **189,000**; 180,000 – 180,000 = **0**
Second Row: –90,000 – (–90,000) = **0**; 18,000 – (–90,000) = **108,000**

Opportunity-Loss Table for Table 4.10

(Freund, William, & Perles, 1993)

Economic conditions are good	189,000	0
There is a recession	0	108,000

Since both columns have zero values, the minimax criterion will be used. Of the two losses, the 108,000 loss is better than the 189,000 loss. Thus, it pays to delay the expansion. A manager may consider this decision a better option.

Net Present Value and Future Values of Money

Usually, costs are directly understood as money other than time or trade-off. When individuals make choices involving costs, they think about money. In this case, an important concept on the present value of money is useful in properly calculating costs.

One fundamental measure in assessing what projects, along with the many other alternative projects, pay the highest is to calculate the net present value of the capital for the project. The net present value measures the current at-par worth of the money at hand, discounted at a certain interest rate. The opposite, or its reverse idea, is the future value. The future value is the projected worth of the money that is paid in the future for an interest rate.

Example 4.11. If $1,000 pays $1,331 in three years at an interest rate of 10 percent, the future value of $1,000 at terminal period is $1,331 and the present value of $1,331 is $1,000.

Net Present Value = $FV/(1 + r)^t$

Where FV = future value at time t; r = interest rate; t = time

In the example,

$$\text{Net Present Value} = \frac{1331}{(1+1.10)^3}$$

$$\text{NPV} = \$1,000$$

Future Value = $PV(1 + r)^t$

In the example,
Future Value = $1,000(1 + 0.10)^3$

Future Value = $1,331

The decision rule is to **accept the project having the highest NPV.** Factors that affect NPV are the rate of interest and time. If the interest rate (i) is high, the NPV is low. If it takes long to realize a terminal value (t), the NPV is low. Therefore, it pays to make the interest rate (i) low and the terminal period (t) short.

Example 4.12. Given a $1,000 investment in different offers, which one is best?

Offer 1: Repayment of $1,331 in four years at 10 percent
Offer 2: Repayment of $1,331 in three years at 6 percent
Offer 3: Repayment of $1,331 in three years at 10 percent

Solution

Offer 1: NPV = $1,331/(1 + 0.10)^4$ = $909.09
Offer 2: NVP = $1,331/(1 + 0.06)3$ = $1,117.49
Offer 3: NVP = $1,331/(1 + 0.10)^3$ = $1,000.00

Since offer 2 has the highest NPV, it pays to invest in it. Offer 2 offers the lowest interest and its terminal value is realized the earliest.

Steps in Excel

1. Open Excel environment. Click the *fx* button. On the **Search for a function,** window, write **NPV.** Select **NPV** from **Select a function.** Click **OK**
2. Enter the rate in decimal orientation, such as 0.10 for 10 percent in example 1.
3. Enter the values in array. Zero value on the second window, zero value on the third window and 1331 on the fourth window representing the third year.
4. The sequence will be 0, 0, 1331). Click **OK.**

The Excel picture would look like the following:

Example 4.13

A student wants to sell his laptop computer, and he received two offers. The first consists of a full payment of ₱15,000.00, and the second offer consists of three payments. One is a down payment of ₱8,000.00, and the remaining two instalments would consist of a ₱5,000.00 payment after six months and ₱2,400.00 after twelve months. The money is assumed to earn an interest rate of 10 percent annually. Which option is better?

The traditional common-sense decision-making process is to compare the total nominal returns carried by two options—₱15,000 and ₱15,400. However, when time dimension is incorporated, cost of money per unit time will also be part of the process. Here, the interest rate of 10 percent might provide the decision-maker a different perspective. The table that follows summarizes the transactions and compares the true values of the two nominal money returns.

Mode of Payments	Nominal Cash Out	Present Value at 10%	Present Value
A. Full Payment Now			**₱15,000.00**
B. Instalments			
Down payment	₱8,000.00	₱8,000.00	
2nd payment	₱5,000.00	₱4,761.90	
Last payment	₱2,400.00	₱2,181.82	
Total	**₱15,400.00**		
Total Present Value			**₱14,943.72**

In order to valuate returns, present values of future returns are calculated. The formula is given by equation 1.

$$(1) \quad PV(M) = \frac{\textbf{money received in the future } R}{(1 + i)}$$

The interpretation of the table is as follows:

a. The present value of the down payment ₱8,000.00 is also ₱8,000.00.
b. The present value of ₱5,000 after six months is **₱4,761.90,** found by 5,000/1.05, since half the year is half the interest.
c. The present value of the last payment is **₱2,181.82,** found by 2,400/1.10, since the annual interest rate is 10 percent.
d. By adding all the values, the total present value under the instalment scheme is **₱14,943.72** only. This is less than when the payment is made in cash, even if nominally it amounts to ₱15,400.00.
e. The optimal decision for the student is to have the payment in cash.

Steps in Excel

1. Click **fx.** Choose **NPV.**
2. Enter 0.05 in the **Interest Rate** (half of the year).
3. Enter 5,000 in the **First Value.** Click **OK.**
4. The answer must be $4,761.90.

5. Do the same for the $2,400 value. The **NPV** must be $2,181.82.
6. Add all NPV values—**$4,761.90, $2,181.82,** and **$8,000.00**—and the total amount is **$14,943.72**

Risks and Returns

E xpected risks are calculated in terms of expected costs, and expected returns are measured with respect to expected benefits. The two are simply the mirror image of each other. When risks are low, beneficial outcomes are expectedly large, and if risks are high, perceived beneficial outcomes are outweighed by their costs. Hence, the rates of return measurements (A-) are the complements of the rates of risk measurements (A). Stock-market investment generally has the following expected rate-of-returns equation:

$$\text{Expected rate of return} \sum_{i=1}^{n} = Pi \, Ki \text{ where}$$

Pi = are probabilities of occurrence
Ki = are the (yields + capital gain or loss) rates

Example 4.14. Given two investment options where the investor gains interest incomes on both, the table that follows shows the respective picture of the returns and the probabilities on demand strengths. Which investment option should the investor put his money in?

Economic conditions	A Company's return given economic conditions	B Company's return given the economic conditions	Probability of demand given economic conditions
Strong	100	30	0.3
Weak	(70)	15	0.4
Normal	15	20	0.3
Total			1.0

Solution

For Company A

$100(0.3) + (-70)(0.4) + 15(0.3) = 6.5\%$

The expected rate of return is 6.5 percent.

For Company B

$30(0.3) + 15(0.4) + 20(0.3) = 21\%$

The expected rate of return is 21 percent for company B.

For this, investment should flow towards company B. In the case of government projects, however, some reconsiderations may be incorporated into the decision structure. When governments spend money for economic development and social services, it is imperative to consider the risks it takes and the returns it enjoys over time. Thus, expectations and the concept of probability may be incorporated in the analysis of costs and benefits. Normally, project costs are incurred over a shorter period, but social gains are earned over a longer period.

In considering social projects, the fundamental target equilibrium scenario for optimum condition is that the marginal benefit the society enjoys for a particular public good or service should be at least equal to the marginal costs of providing public goods or services. In symbols, the equilibrium condition is expressed by

$$MCg = \Sigma i = a + b \, MB \, {}^{i}g.$$

In particular, there are conditions to meet in order for a social project to be acceptable. These are the following:

1. Benefits are greater than costs. This concerns the social impact of the project. If the beneficial impact is greater than the social costs, then the project is acceptable.
2. Benefits are greater than the opportunity costs. This part of the consideration is concerned with the cost of capital to be used in carrying out the project. If the net present value is greater than the cost of borrowing or of the opportunity cost of capital, the project is considered.

3. For mutually exclusive admissible projects with positive net present values (NPV), the rule is to choose the project having the highest NPV.
4. For admissible projects that can be jointly undertaken, the rule is to choose the combination of projects that generates the highest NPV.

Internal Rate of Returns

A nother criterion on whether the project should be taken involves the internal rate of returns (IRR). The IRR should be larger than the opportunity costs of capital (OCC). The OCC is the value of the next best alternative forgone in favour of the accepted project. This means that if the approved project has a calculated return of 12 percent, the government should not be getting a higher investment return elsewhere but on the project approved.

Internal rate of return (ρ) is defined as the percentage that finds equality between the invested capital and its returns, such that

$$-1_a + \frac{FV}{(1+p)} = 0$$

Where *Ia = initial investment*
  FV = future value
  P = *internal rate of return*

Example 4.15. If the government spends $1M today on an advertising campaign and reaps a benefit of $1.04M in revenue a year from now, what is the IRR?

Solution

  −1,000,000 + 1,040,000/(1 + ρ) = 0
  1,040,000/(1 + ρ) = 1,000,000; 1,000,000(1 + ρ) = 1,040,000
  1,000,000ρ + 1,000,000 = 1,040,000;
  1,000,000p = 1,040,000 − 1,000,000; P = 40,000/1,000,000
    P = 4%, which is actually the rate of increase in profit.

Investment Criteria and the Appropriate Discount Rate

For a project to be acceptable, two conditions need to be met. These are that *benefits exceed costs* and *benefits exceed opportunity costs*. Since the money used to finance big projects is borrowed, these are subject to interest rates, the cost of capital. When the economy is fully monetized, the interest rate could proxy well the opportunity cost of capital, but since some countries have control over the domestic banking system, interest rates are held fixed, and therefore varying rates may not be a better estimate. What then is the appropriate discount rate?

Countries solve this issue by taking the weighted average of the real return on investment and interest rates on fixed deposits with commercial banks, and they have established the rate to fall from 10 percent to 15 percent. This means that projects with a real return of 10 to 15 percent are considered economically viable.

A social project has an internal rate of return (ρ) that solves the equation.

$$B_0 - C_0 \frac{B_1 - C_1}{1+p} + \frac{B_2 - C_2}{(1+p)^2} + \dots \frac{B_{T-C_T}}{(1+p)^T} = 0$$

Rule: Accept the project if ρ > firm's opportunity cost of funds (i).

In most cases, however, decisions concerning returns of government projects are not based on a simple, arbitrary fixed rate like 10 to 15 percent. Another approximation is to calculate NPV on two possible interest rates. The example is presented below (Kholi 1993).

Example 4.16.

Economic Internal Rate of Return
(in Million Pesos)

Year	Cash Flow
	B-C
0	-9000
1	-2000
2	1000
3	4000
4	4000
5	4000
6	4000
7	4000
8	4000
9	2000
at 12% NPV =	$3,431.30
at 20% NPV=	($289.23)

When the discount factor is at 12 percent, the NPV of the project adds up to $3,431.30. When the discount factor is raised to 20 percent, the NPV returns a negative value. This means that the true EIRR of the project must be between 12 percent and 20 percent. The problem is to find out the best EIRR approximate value.

Steps in Excel

1. Enter the cash-flow data in one column. Choose an empty cell anywhere.
2. Click **fx**. Choose **NPV.** On the first window, enter 0.12 for a 12 percent rate.
3. On the second window, highlight the data by dragging through the entire column.
4. Click **OK.** The answer must by 3,431. This is the NPV of the array given the 12 percent rate.
5. Do the same with the 20 percent rate. The NPV is (289.23).

Steps in Recalculating a Better EIRR Approximation (Kholi 1993)

1. Calculate the two NPV: 12% = 3,431.30 and 20% = (289.23).
2. Find their difference: 3,431.30 – (–289.23) = $3,720.53.
3. Divide the NPV at the lower interest rate to the value computed in number 2.
4. 3,431.30/3,720.53 = 0.922260075. This will now become the factor.
5. Multiply this factor by the difference in interest rate for 8 percent: (20% – 12%); 8 * 0.922260075 = 7.37808056.
6. Add this to the lower interest rate of 12 percent (12% + 7.37808056 = 19.37 . . . %).
7. The EIRR of the project is 19 percent.

Benefit-Cost Analysis

The benefit-cost ratio calculates the magnitudes of benefits per unit cost through the calculation of the respective net present values. It adheres to the following equations:

$$NPV_B = B_0 + \frac{B_1}{(1+i)} + \frac{B_2}{(1+i)^2} + \cdots + \frac{B_T}{(1+i)^T}$$

$$NPV_C = C + \frac{C_1}{(1+i)} + \frac{C_2}{(1+i)^2} + \cdots + \frac{C_T}{(1+i)^T}$$

Rule: The computed B-C ratio should be greater than (>) 1. This means that the benefits of the project outweigh the costs of that project.

The Best Decision Guide

The NPV is considered the best decision guide. Take two projects. Project A requires $100 and yielding $110 a year from now on. And project B is spending $1,000, yielding $1,080 in a year. Assume that a firm can borrow and lend freely at 6 percent annually (Rosen 1988). Which project should be taken?

Solution

Project A: $110/100 =1.1$ or 10 percent increase, meaning IRR of 10 percent.
Deduct the cost of funds at 6%: 10% – 6% = 4%
Real internal rate of return = 4%
Real Actual Value: $4

Project B: $1,080/1,000 = 1.08 or 8 percent increase, meaning IRR of 8 percent.
Deduct the cost of capital at 6%: 8% – 6% = 2%
Real rate of return = 2%
Real Actual Value: $20 (found by $1,080 – $1,000 = $80: $1,000 * 0.06 = $60; deduct 60 from 80, $80 – $60 = $20)

On the basis of the IRR, obviously, project A should be chosen because it registers a higher IRR than project B. However, based on the real actual value, project B makes a higher return. Thus, IRR is a poor guide criterion for investments.

On the other hand, the benefit-cost ratio is a poor guide to investment as well. Think of a community that is considering two methods for disposing of toxic wastes. Method A is a toxic-waste dump with benefits that total $250M and costs that equal $100M. The benefit-cost ratio is 2.5. Method B involves sending the wastes in a rocket to Neptune with benefits equalling $200M and costs equalling $100M (Rosen 1988). The benefit-cost ratio is 2. Comparing the two values, method A is chosen over method B because it entails more benefits than costs.

However, the analyst missed including in the valuation the costs accrued to the environment in the first method. This missed value amounted to $40M.

If this value is viewed as a reduction to benefit, then the B-C ratio is (250 – 40)/100 = 210/100 = 2.1. If this is, however, viewed as an increase in cost, then B-C would be 250/140 = 1.78, which is now lower than method B. It has now appeared that throwing garbage to Neptune is a more beneficial garbage disposal project between the two. The confusion lies therefore on the treatment of the environmental cost. Should it be viewed as a reduction in benefit or an increase in cost?

Example 4.17. The following are the data on costs and benefits cash flows of project A and project B at 10 percent. Calculate NPV. What project may be implemented?

Project A @ 10 Percent

Years	Benefits ($)	Costs ($)	Cash Flows ($) (B-C)
1	-	5000	-5000
2	2000	1000	1000
3	3000	1000	2000
4	4000	1000	3000
5	5000	1000	4000
Total	14000	9000	5000

Solution: NPV = **$2,316**

Steps in Excel

a. Click **fx.** Choose the **NPV** button.
b. Enter the rate on the first window, and enter all the enumerated values under the benefits column. Click **Enter,** and the value is registered on the cell.
c. Repeat the procedure to perform the same for the cost stream.
d. Deduct cost stream value from the benefit stream value, and the NPV is calculated.

Project B @ 10 Percent

Years	Benefits ($)	Costs ($)	Cash Flows (B-C) (S)
1	1000	2000	-1000
2	2000	2000	0
3	4000	2000	2000
4	4000	2000	2000
5	4000	2000	2000
	15000	10000	5000

Solution
NPV = **$3,201**

On the basis of the NPV, it is preferable to implement project B. It has a higher net present value.

Net Present Values on Costs across Years

M any big projects have costs spread over years, and finding the net present value of these projects requires inclusion of time. Take the following example.

Example 4.18.
The economic cost of a $12,000 food-processing project is spread over two years. The table below shows the spread of the stream of costs and benefits for nine years at 12 percent (Kholi 1993). Use Excel to calculate NPV.

Year	Benefit	Cost	B-C
0	0	9000	-9000
1	0	2000	-2000
2	2000	1000	1000
3	4000	0	4000
4	4000	0	4000
5	4000	0	4000
6	4000	0	4000
7	4000	0	4000
8	4000	0	4000
9	2000	0	2000

Solution

1. In Excel environment, on the **fx** window, type the following commands: = NPV(0.12,0,0,2000,4000,4000,4000,4000,4000, 4000,2000) for "benefits" data
2. Do the same for "costs" data.
3. Deduct the values on costs from those in the benefits.
4. The result is **$3,431.30.**
5. This resulting figure is the NPV value.

Excel Environment on Calculating NPV of a Food-Processing Project

The cell formula shown: =NPV(0.12,0,0,2000,4000,4000,4000,4000,4000,2000)

	Benefit	Cost	Benefit-Cost
	$13,773.18	$10,341.88	$3,431.30

Year	Benefit	Cost	B-C
0	0	9000	-9000
1	0	2000	-2000
2	2000	1000	1000
3	4000	0	4000
4	4000	0	4000
5	4000	0	4000
6	4000	0	4000
7	4000	0	4000
8	4000	0	4000
9	2000	0	2000
NPV		3431.298775	

Forecasting

When data are in time series, one possibility of its use is in forecasting. In business, it is important to have a picture of what is going to happen in the market. A simple forecast can be implemented to project future values not yet realized but which are of equal importance with those already realized.

Example 4.19. Pendley Corporation (Weida 2001) intends to forecast its future demand using historical demand for the last six years. Make a forecast for the seventh year. The data are as follows:

Table 4.19 Actual Historical Demand for the Past Six Years, Pendley Corporation

Years	Quarters	Demand
1	1.00	3.47
	2.00	3.12
	3.00	3.97
	4.00	4.50
2	5.00	4.06
	6.00	6.90
	7.00	3.60
	8.00	6.47
3	9.00	4.27
	10.00	5.24
	11.00	6.39
	12.00	5.45
4	13.00	5.88
	14.00	8.99
	15.00	4.12
	16.00	6.68
5	17.00	9.44
	18.00	7.75
	19.00	9.91
	20.00	9.14
6	21.00	14.25
	22.00	14.89
	23.00	14.22
	24.00	15.56

Procedures

1. Enter data. Click **Data** button, choose **Data Analysis** and click **Regression**. In the **Input Y Range** window, enter the data set of "Demand". In the **Input X Range** input the data under "Quarters"

2. Identify the intercept and the slope value. For this example, the intercept is **1.495254** and the slope is the value next to "quarters" variable of **0.474613**. Kindly refer to table 4.20.

Table 4.20 Regression Summary of Actual Demand in Table 4.19

Regression Statistics	
Multiple R	0.865564546
R Square	0.749201983
Adjusted R Square	0.737802073
Standard Error	1.985362614
Observations	24

ANOVA					
	df	SS	MS	F	Significance F
Regression	1	259.0462	259.0462	65.71999	4.73353E-08
Residual	22	86.71662	3.941665		
Total	23	345.7628			

	Coefficients	Standard Error	t Stat	P value
Intercept	**1.495253623**	0.836534	1.78744	0.087652
Quarters	**0.474613043**	0.058545	8.106787	4.73E-08

3. Make another column. Name this new column as the fitted demand or the forecasted demand. Calculate the fitted demand using this equation: intercept + (slope*quarter's variable). In this example, in the first cell, it is (1.495254 + 0.474613 * 1). The answer is 1.97.

4. For the second cell, it is (1.495254 + 0.474613 * 2). The answer is 2.44.

5. Do the same for the rest of the values down the array.

6. In the "quarters" column, add four quarters. This is for the seventh-year forecast. Extend the equation to compute the fitted demand for these quarters.

7. The **added values** are the **forecast demand** using historical data, assuming that there are no changes in the slope and the intercept.

8. The results appear in table 4.21 in red and in larger fonts.
9. The graphical presentation of the forecast is in chart 4.18.

Table 4.21

Quarters	Demand	Fitted Demand
1.00	3.47	1.97
2.00	3.12	2.44
3.00	3.97	2.92
4.00	4.50	3.39
5.00	4.06	3.87
6.00	6.90	4.34
7.00	3.60	4.82
8.00	6.47	5.29
9.00	4.27	5.77
10.00	5.24	6.24
11.00	6.39	6.72
12.00	5.45	7.19
13.00	5.88	7.67
14.00	8.99	8.14
15.00	4.12	8.61
16.00	6.68	9.09
17.00	9.44	9.56
18.00	7.75	10.04
19.00	9.91	10.51
20.00	9.14	10.99
21.00	14.25	11.46
22.00	14.89	11.94
23.00	14.22	12.41
24.00	15.56	12.89
25.00		**13.36**
26.00		**13.84**
27.00		**14.31**
28.00		**14.78**

Chart 4.18a Actual and Fitted Demand Given a Derived Slope and an Intercept

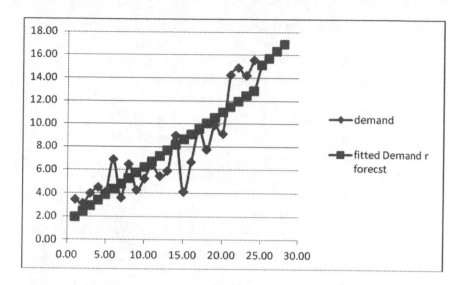

The forecast demand is lower than the actual trend. In case there are doubts about the forecast, changes in the slope and intercept perceived to be more fitting may be encoded to the equation. The resulting forecast values will change. For instance, the management has a strong intuition that the slope is 0.62 and the intercept is –0.40. The forecast for the seventh year will change. See chart 4.18b. Note that the actual and the forecast converge.

Essential to forecasting is the measure of confidence. One more commonality is the mean square error (MSE). This value should be small, implying that the forecast and the actual difference should be almost zero.

To calculate for the MSE,

a. get the difference between the actual and the fitted,
b. square this difference, and
c. average the squared difference and get the square root. The answer is 1.9.

Steps in Excel in Finding MSE

1. Make a fourth column and name it squared difference. On the first cell, click = to denote making a formula; then highlight the first cell under the fitted demand, click the minus sign (-), and highlight the first cell of the actual demand.
2. Click the circumflex accent (^) and write 2. Press **Enter.** This is now the squared deviation.
3. The answer in the first cell is 2.25. Copy this formula and paste to the cells down the array.
4. Highlight the entire fourth column with values and click **Average** in the capital letter sigma (Σ) cluster under the **Editing** group. The answer is 3.61.
5. Click the **fx** button and choose **SQRT.** On the window, enter the cell that contains the 3.61 value. The answer must be 1.9.

Chart 4.18b Actual and Fitted Demand Given a Changed Slope and Intercept

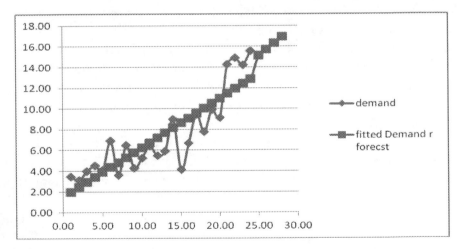

Achieving Desired Outcomes

I n most industrial cases, an objective target is an important guide. Excel can likewise help a new administrator or manager achieve a goal.

Example 4.20. Suppose a small school has the following data. What possible decisions must the administration take in order to achieve a profit of ₱1,000,000 at the end of the following year?

Months	No. of Students	Monthly Fees	Monthly Income	Staff Expense	Rent Expense	Other Costs	Total Costs
January	50	2000	100000	20000	30000	15000	65000
February	55	2000	110000	20000	30000	15000	65000
March	50	2000	100000	20000	30000	15000	65000
April	60	2000	120000	20000	30000	15000	65000
May	50	2000	100000	20000	30000	15000	65000
June	70	2000	140000	20000	30000	15000	65000
July	70	2000	140000	20000	30000	15000	65000
August	60	2000	120000	20000	30000	15000	65000
September	50	2000	100000	20000	30000	15000	65000
October	50	2000	100000	20000	30000	15000	65000
November	50	2000	100000	20000	30000	15000	65000
December	50	2000	100000	20000	30000	15000	65000
Annual Totals	665	24000	1330000				780000

Steps in Excel

1. Enter the data in a worksheet.
2. Calculate the annual income and the annual expenses.
3. In other cells, put the total income and expenses information.
4. Deduct expenses from income values to calculate the profit.
5. The current profit is only ₱550,000, and the objective is to make this ₱1,000,000 the following year.
6. The results are in the following table.

Months	No. of Students	Monthly Fees	Monthly Income	Staff Expense	Rent Expense	Other Costs	Total Costs
January	50	2000	100000	20000	30000	15000	65000
February	55	2000	110000	20000	30000	15000	65000
March	50	2000	100000	20000	30000	15000	65000
April	60	2000	120000	20000	30000	15000	65000
May	50	2000	100000	20000	30000	15000	65000
June	70	2000	140000	20000	30000	15000	65000
July	70	2000	140000	20000	30000	15000	65000
August	60	2000	120000	20000	30000	15000	65000
September	50	2000	100000	20000	30000	15000	65000
October	50	2000	100000	20000	30000	15000	65000
November	50	2000	100000	20000	30000	15000	65000
December	50	2000	100000	20000	30000	15000	65000
Totals	665	24000	1330000				780000

Annual	**Income**	**1330000**
Annual	**Expenses**	**780000**
	Profit	**550000**

7. Click on the cell with the 550,000.00 value and click **Data.** In the data group, choose **Solver.** (Install this first, if not installed.)
8. The **Set Target Cell** window is highlighted.
9. On the **Equal To**, click **Value Of** and enter **1000000** on the window.
10. Under the **By Changing Cells**, highlight the columns on **Number of Students, Monthly Fees and Other Costs.** This means that these are the cells you want to change.
11. On the **Subject to the Constraints** window, click **Add** and highlight the number of students, and then choose **Integer.** This means that you require the number of students to be whole numbers.
12. Click **Add** again, highlight the **Number of Students** column, and define it to be less than or equal to 70. (≤70 implies that the maximum number of students would be 70.)

13. Click **Add** again, highlight the **Other Costs** column, and set it to less than or equal to 15,000 (≤15,000 implies that the maximum other costs will be 15,000).

14. Click **Add** again, highlight the **Other Costs** column, and set it to greater than or equal to 13,500 (≥ 13,500 implies that the minimum value of other costs will be 13,500).

15. In effect, the other costs will vary between 13,500 and 15,000.

16. The results are as follows:

17. Click **Solve.**

Months	No. of Students	Monthly Fees	Monthly Income	Staff Expense	Rent Expense	Other Costs	Total Costs
January	70	2119.006	148330.4168	20000	30000	15000	65000
February	70	2119.056	148333.9165	20000	30000	15000	65000
March	70	2119.006	148330.4168	20000	30000	15000	65000
April	70	2119.093	148336.5414	20000	30000	15000	65000
May	70	2119.006	148330.4168	20000	30000	15000	65000
June	70	2119.143	148340.0414	20000	30000	15000	65000
July	70	2119.143	148340.0414	20000	30000	15000	65000
August	70	2119.093	148336.5414	20000	30000	15000	65000
September	70	2119.006	148330.4168	20000	30000	15000	65000
October	70	2119.006	148330.4168	20000	30000	15000	65000
November	70	2119.006	148330.4168	20000	30000	15000	65000
December	70	2119.006	148330.4168	20000	30000	15000	65000
Totals	840	25428.57	1780000				780000

Annual	Income	1780000
Annual	Expenses	780000
	Profit	1000000

The results serve as the guide to the manager. The table says that with costs not changing anything in order to earn ₱1,000,000 profit the next year, the total number of students must be seventy. The full capacity level and the monthly payment per student should be raised to ₱2,119.006.

Bibliography

Bibliography

Answers.com (n.d.). *Normal Distributions.* Retrieved from www. answers. com: http://ph.images.search.yahoo.com/images.

Connally, E., D. Hughes-Hallett, A. Gleason, et al. "Fitting Curves to Data." *Functions Modeling Change: A Preparation for Calculus.* USA: John Wiley and Sons, Inc., 1998.

Cozby, Paul. *Methods of Behavioural Research.* California: Mayfield Publishing Company, 1997.

Freund, J. E., F. J. Williams, and B. M. Perles. *Elementary Business Statistics: The Modern Approach.* New Jersey: Prentice Hall, Inc., 1993.

Freund, J. E. *Elementary Business Statistics.* New Jersey: 1982.

Freund, J. E., and F. J. Williams. *Elementary Business Statistics.* New Jersey: 1982.

Gujarati, D. *Essentials of Econometrics, 2nd ed.* Singapore: Irwin/McGraw-Hill, 1999.

Gujarati, Damodar. *Essentials of Econometrics, 2nd ed. A Review of Basic Statistical Concepts.* Singapore: McGraw-Hill, 1999.

http://ph.images.search.yahoo.com/search/images (n.d.). Retrieved from http://ph.images.search.yahoo.com/search/images.

Freund, J., William, F., & Perles, B. (1993). The Maximin and Maximax Criterion. In J. Freund, F. William, & B. Perles, *Elementary Business Statistics: the Modern Approach* (p. 208). New Jersey: Prentice Hall.

Levine, D. M. "Basic Probability and Discrete Probability Distribution." *Statistics for Managers Using Microsoft Excel.* New Jersey: Prentice Hall, Inc., 1999.

Levine, David M., Mark L. Berenson, and David Stephan. "Decision Making." *Statistics for Managers Using Microsoft Excel 2nd ed.* Prentice Hall International, Inc., 1999.

Statistics How To (n.d.). *How to Calculate Normal Distribution Probability in Excel.* Retrieved June 10, 2013, from http://www.statisticshowto.com/blog.

Wackerly, D. D. "The Hypergeometric Probability Distribution." *Mathematical Statistics with Applications, 7th ed.* Canada: Thomson Learning, Inc., 2008.

Walpole, R. E. "Hypergeometric Distribution." *Probability and Statistics for Engineers and Scientists, 5th ed.* New York: Macmillan Publishing Company, 1993.

Weida, N. R. "Advanced Forecasting." *Operations Analysis Using Microsoft Excel.* California: Duxbury Thompson Learning, 2001.

Anderson, D. R., Sweeney, D. J., & Williams, T. A. (2006). *Modern Business Statistics with Microsoft Excel, 2e.* China: Thompson South-Western.

Asian Development Bank. (various years). *Key Indicators for Asia and the Pacific.* ADB.

Balino, A., & Bangero, I. e. (2010). *Various Fish Markets for Iloilo Fish Supply.* Iloilo City: unpublished thesis.

Freund, J. E., & J., W. F. (1977). *Elementary Business Statistics: The Modern Approach.* Prentice Hall.

NetMBA Business Knowledge Center. (n.d.). *The Normal Distribution (Bell Curve).* Retrieved February 6, 2013, from NetMBA Business Knowledge Center: http://www.netmba.com/statistics/distribution/normal/

Polit, D. F., & Bernadette, H. (1995). *Nursing Research: Principles and Methods, 5 ed.* Philadelphia: JB Lippincott Company.